Pistol in the Pulpit

A biblical and tactical response to active shooters in the house of worship

Foreword by Joery Smittick, Deputy Chief (retired) San Antonio Police Department

Tim Rupp

Printed by Snowfall Press
snowfallpress.com

"I highly recommend Pastor Tim's book 'Pistol in the Pulpit' for any church considering or developing a security team and also for any Christian who wants to know what the Bible has to say about self-defense for themselves, their family and friends. Tim has covered all of the bases for anyone wanting to educate themselves on biblical principles for self-defense as well as weapon selection, training, self-defense actions, and mindset."

—Doug Dryden, Owner and lead instructor at Highlands Tactical Training Group, Plains, Montana

"With a law enforcement officer's training and a pastor's heart, Dr. Tim Rupp weaves Biblical insight, training, tactics, personal experiences and recommendations into a great read on why each church should have multiple Safety Response Teams. You will be riveted by his writing and challenged by his leading you and your church to action to increase the security awareness at your facility. Tim's balanced approach, real-world experience and active engagement in the church he currently pastors brings to life the need for that of which he writes!"

—Rev. Jonathan Wiggins, Rocky Mountain District, The Christian and Missionary Alliance

"This book is a must read for anyone considering or already operating a security program in a Christian environment. It was obvious early on that I was following the pen of one who had been there – spiritually, mentally and physically. Tim Rupp has the DNA of a protector and the heart of a pastor.

He understands faith-based principles of protection and presents them well. I couldn't find one thing to disagree with. His use of scriptural and life examples throughout provided applicable lessons learned I will never forget."

—Carl Chinn, Faith-based security professional,
Author of *Evil Invades Sanctuary*

"Practical applications, along with personal vignettes, and appropriate case studies make this book applicable to law enforcement, church leadership, or anyone concerned with protection of vulnerable targets."

—Joery Smittick, Deputy Chief (retired)
San Antonio Police Department

"Tim Rupp's amazing and critically important monograph Pistol in the Pulpit brings thoughtfulness, understanding, wisdom, and Scripture to bear on an important issue of our era. Ardent proponents of carrying handguns too often show more macho than they do wisdom. On the other hand, the left-leaning social order seems almost content to do little more than cry for gun control when innocents are killed. But Rupp comprehends the gravity of the whole dilemma and counsels a course that will save lives, sometimes even those of the aggressors. There is not a pastor, a Board of Elders, or a diaconate who should fail to read this book and act accordingly."

—Dr. Paige Patterson, President Southwestern Baptist
Theological Seminary, Fort Worth, Texas

Pistol in the Pulpit

A biblical and tactical response to active shooters in the house of worship

by Tim Rupp

KDP ISBN: 9781519073181

Author Contact Info: office@ruppshooting.com

Rupp Shooting Academy
Idaho Falls, ID
ruppshooting.com

Pistol in the Pulpit

Preface

Norman Rockwell captured twentieth century Americana in his iconic paintings that appeared on the front cover of the Saturday Evening Post for nearly fifty years. But as the century came to a close, America turned a new page. Rockwell died in 1978 and the American culture as we knew it died shortly thereafter. The tipping point came in 1999 with the Columbine High School massacre. Mass murders of innocent people in public places is now an understood reality.

The twenty-first century saw the paintings of Rockwell replaced by images of shootings in the public square at schools, malls, and houses of worship. For the first time in American history the threat of violence is dominated by the fear of a domestic attack rather than a foreign one.

What is the biblical approach to this threat? Christians are struggling with how to respond. Do we trust God and pray for his protection? Do we "turn the other cheek" and do nothing when someone threatens to kill us? Do we take up arms to defend ourselves and others? Sometimes an illegal physical assault or threatened attack is confused with Christian persecution—the act of a government attempting to silence people from preaching the gospel by arrest, prison, and/or torture as experienced by the first century church and modern churches in many nations around the world, today. However, persecution for preaching the gospel and an illegal physical assault by an individual(s) acting outside the law are distinct issues that call for equally distinct responses.

While Christians commonly protect themselves from physical assaults using nonlethal force, we must understand that employing lethal force is far different. Utilizing a force that will likely result in serious bodily injury, or even the death of another human, is not to be taken lightly. Believers who take up arms to protect themselves or others must be

i

prepared spiritually, mentally, and tactically. Without proper preparation in all three of these critical areas the outcome, both immediately and afterwards, may prove disastrous. The ability to quickly, effectively, and safely deploy lethal force to save innocent lives requires more than a passing familiarity with a firearm and the license to wield it.

Christians who choose the responsibility of employing lethal force must be informed by both a spiritual and tactical foundation. Not only is there a proper biblical response, there is also a proper tactical response. What are these proper responses? These critical questions are answered in the pages that follow.

Tim Rupp
April, 2016

Dedication

To my fallen brother and sister officers who stood in the gap and to my fellow keepers of our Lord's sheep.

Special thanks to Mrs. Trisha Randall for her editing.

Table of Contents

Foreword

Active-shooting incidents are increasingly a part of daily news broadcasts worldwide. Shopping malls, military bases, colleges, elementary, middle, and high schools—every place is susceptible to an active-shooter incident. Even the place where people go to find peace—the house of God—is vulnerable to the rampages of violence.

I have known Tim Rupp for over thirty years; we worked alongside each other as patrol officers, detectives, and training academy staff members. Most importantly, I can attest with confidence that Tim is my brother in Christ. All the work he does is inspired to glorify the name of Jesus.

Tim is uniquely qualified to produce this very timely book. His law enforcement career spans over twenty years. He has acted as an instructor in many areas of law enforcement training including firearms, tactics, and physical training. Tim also served as a detective where he investigated murders and officer-involved shootings.

God's Word prescribes a balanced approach to our understanding of self-defense. In Nehemiah 4:9, the workers on the wall had tools and weapons as they worked. Jesus told his disciples, "I am sending you out like sheep among wolves. Therefore be as shrewd as snakes and as innocent as doves" (Matthew 10:16, NIV). Tim's stellar law enforcement career provides a great deal of insight into this balanced approach. But Tim is also currently serving as a senior pastor. It is the rare combination of skills, experience, and God-ordained calling that allows Tim to produce this holistic and thorough safety plan for places of worship.

Practical applications, along with personal vignettes, and appropriate case studies make this book applicable to law enforcement, church leadership, or anyone concerned with protection of vulnerable targets.

Joery Smittick, Deputy Chief (retired)
San Antonio Police Department

Deputy Chief Smittick is a retired San Antonio Police Officer with 33 years of law enforcement experience. The majority of his career was in patrol and training. He holds a Master of Science in criminal justice leadership and is a graduate of the FBI National Academy.

"If possible, so far as it depends on you, live peaceably with all." (Romans 12:18)

A New America
Chapter 1

A New Normal

"I didn't know what to do or say. I was just numb,"[1] the tearful woman told the reporter, describing her response to two Muslim extremists who walked into the crowded room wearing black tactical clothing, hiding behind masks, and armed with AR-15 rifles and 9mm pistols. While the woman remained frozen, the two assailants methodically shot, reloaded, and shot again—killing 14 people and injuring nearly two dozen more. The early reports from the December 2, 2015, San Bernardino massacre were that in less than one minute 65-75 bullets were either shot at or into some 80 people gathered for an employee Christmas party. The first police officer arriving on the scene, San Bernardino Police Lt. Mike Madden, said that even with his training and experience he wasn't prepared for the incredible carnage caused by the married couple turned assassins.[2]

---

[1] (Live interview of unidentified victim of the San Bernardino shooting, Fox News, December 3, 2015)
[2] (Live police press conference, December 3, 2015)

America is changing before our eyes—the change became apparent in 1999. Maryland's Montgomery County Police Chief Thomas Manger says the 1999 Columbine High School massacre in Colorado was "a wake-up call" for Americans. Chief Manger reports that,

> First, unlike other high-profile crimes with multiple victims, the Columbine massacre did not involve criminals whose motive was financial profit, terrorists trying to obtain the release of their imprisoned brethren, or political radicals or zealots. The Columbine shooters' motivations were not the motives of "traditional" criminals.
>
> Furthermore, the Columbine shootings shocked the nation because they hit close to home for people who were not accustomed to worrying about violent crime. Columbine was an upper-middle-class suburban high school with a high graduation rate, and large majorities of Columbine graduates went on to college. Thus, unlike the case with many other types of crime, average Americans could not look at the Columbine shooting and dismiss it as something that could never happen in their community.[3]

More and more church leaders, staff members, lay leaders, church boards, and denominational leaders need a resource to help them determine if an armed Safety Response Team is right for their church. I've informally surveyed church leaders, parishioners, and police officers to de-

---

[3] (Police Executive Research Forum, 2014, p. 1)

termine the questions and concerns they have about protecting congregations, guests, and church staff with a trained armed Safety Response Team. While I've informally surveyed for questions, the answers are based on Scripture, thorough research, professional training, and expert opinions. Although I'd never be able to address every question or concern, my hope and prayer is that this book will help answer the most basic questions and be a starting place for your church, synagogue, or house of worship to make decisions concerning the protection of those who come onto your property.

After serving four years active duty as an Air Force Law Enforcement Specialist, I joined the San Antonio, Texas, police department, where I served for 24 years as a patrol officer, detective, and sergeant. For more than twenty years, from the beginning of my police training in 1979, patrol officers (both military and civilian) were trained to secure the perimeter when we were the initial responders to a shooting with possible hostages. After the perimeter was secured and the scene contained, we were to notify the dispatcher and wait for the Special Weapons and Tactics (SWAT) team and hostage negotiators to arrive, which could be several minutes or even hours. On those rare occasions when it was necessary for the first responding patrol officers to immediately enter buildings or houses where it was believed an assailant was located, we were trained to *slowly and methodically* enter and search for the bad guys. But, as Chief Manger said, Columbine was a wake-up call. Police tactics changed. No longer could we hope the bad guys would simply give-up or negotiate for hostages. They weren't coming for hostages—they were coming to kill. Hence, law enforcement needed the first responding officers to enter quickly, ignore injured victims, and stop the killing by engaging the assailant(s).

So if the police are trained to stop active shooters, why do churches need to worry about having an armed

Safety Response Team in place? Why not just call the police? *"Why?"* is a legitimate question when considering the serious issue of having persons armed with firearms to protect a church congregation. Is there a need for such "drastic measures" as some say of armed protection? Or is this just fearmongering? What does the Bible say about deadly force protection? Where does one begin getting a team together? Who should be on the team? Who shouldn't? What about training? What are the personal ramifications of using deadly force and killing another human being? What are some firearm basics that need to be considered?

Responding to the Rise of Violence in Church

Violent acts of aggression in churches are on the increase. *Christianity Today* reports that death from church attacks were up 36% in 2012.[4] Church security consultant Carl Chinn reports that from 1999 to 2015 there were nearly 1,200 deadly force incidents reported at faith-based organizations in America. Faith-based organizations are churches and para-church organizations. These attacks resulted in the deaths of 626 innocent victims.[5]

In a Federal Bureau of Investigation (FBI) study of active-shooter incidents (an incident in which a person is actively engaged in murdering people in populated places) between 2000 and 2013,

> [T]he FBI identified 160 active-shooter incidents, noting they occurred in small and large towns, in urban and rural areas, and in 40 of 50 states and the District of Columbia. Though incidents occurred primarily in commerce and educational environments

---

[4] (Steffan, 2013)
[5] (Chinn, Ministry Violence Statistics, 2016)

(70.0%), they also occurred on city streets, on military and other government properties, and in private residences, health care facilities, and *houses of worship*. The shooters victimized young and old, male and female, family members, and people of all races, cultures, and religions. [Italics added][6]

Homicides at faith-based organizations are trending upwards. From 2009 to 2015 Mr. Chinn reports 426 deadly force deaths, an average of nearly 61 deaths per year.[7] That's more than one per week.

There are places Americans expect to be safe. Home, school, and church have traditionally been three places where we expect our families to be safe from physical harm. We expect children to be able to live, learn, and play without the fear of being harmed or killed. But things have changed.

How we choose to protect our families from harm at home is an individual choice. Americans exercise the right to protect themselves and their families with locks, security systems, and weapons. Americans also enjoy the services of highly trained, competent, and professional law enforcement patrols. However, such professional policing gives people an unrealistic sense of security. It's a false notion for Americans to believe the police will be present to protect them against crime. In fact, you may be surprised to know that the average response time for crimes-in-progress is much longer than people realize. Maybe that's why in first century Rome Jesus spoke of a man protecting his own home. *"When a strong man, fully armed, guards his own palace, his goods are safe,"* (Luke 11:21). Jesus didn't say a man's goods are safe because the Roman army is close by, but because *"a strong man, fully armed"* is there to protect his own home.

---

[6] (Texas State University and Federal Bureau of Investigation, 2014, p. 8)
[7] (Chinn, Ministry Violence Statistics, 2016)

The median police response time to an active-shooter incident is three minutes.[8] That seems rather quick until you realize this is the *median* time, meaning half of the time it takes officers longer than three minutes. Also note this is the time from when officers are dispatched until they arrive on the scene. This doesn't include the time it takes to make the phone call (the median report time is also three minutes)[9] and the time it takes for the dispatcher to get the information needed before dispatching officers. Further, this doesn't include the time it takes for the officers to locate the incident, form a plan, enter, and engage the aggressor. Dr. J. Pete Blair of Texas State University has conducted extensive research on active-shooter incidents and says,

> These events [active-shooter incidents] generally happened very quickly. The most common resolution, in the events that stop before the police arrive, is that the shooter commits suicide. What we tend to see is that the attackers have an initial burst of violence. They have so many victims in front of them; they attack those victims; they run out of victims; and they kill themselves.[10]

Note that in the San Bernardino massacre the assailants departed prior to police arriving and were intent on either returning to intentionally engage police or finding a secondary target while police resources were busy at the first scene.

The above cited FBI study revealed that,

---

8 (Bonneville County Sheriff's Office Active Shooter Training Course)
9 (Bonneville County Sheriff's Office Active Shooter Training Course)
10 (Police Executive Research Forum, 2014, p. 4)

44 (70%) of 63 incidents [where the deration of the event could be ascertained] ended in 5 minutes or less, with 23 ending in 2 minutes or less. Even when law enforcement was present or able to respond within minutes, civilians often had to make life and death decisions, and, therefore, should be engaged in training and discussions on decisions they may face."[11]

In the San Bernardino massacre the first two officers were on the scene in about one minute from the time the call went out, but when they arrived the two assailants had already caused all the bloodshed.

The fact of the matter is, policing is far more reactive than proactive. Reactive policing is reacting to calls for help—a citizen dials 911 and police are notified to respond. Proactive policing is attempting to prevent crime by using intelligence collected to increase patrols, stakeout a likely spot to stop a crime before it

> The fact of the matter is, policing is far more reactive than proactive.

can be completed, or to set up a sting operation where criminals are afforded the opportunity to engage in a crime. The key to proactive policing is gathering intelligence. When the police are able to obtain information about active shooters, their plots to murder can be easily foiled. One problem is a lack of intelligence. The lack of intelligence isn't because police aren't trying, it's that the police are limited. The police have limited resources with an ever-increasing number of people to watch.

---

[11] (Texas State University and Federal Bureau of Investigation, 2014, p. 8)

Perhaps the biggest growing threat is the Islamic State of Iran and Syria (ISIS). As of this writing the FBI has nearly 1,000 open ISIS investigations, with at least one ISIS investigation underway in each of the 50 states. Furthermore, ISIS is actively recruiting young people in the United States to join their cause. Recently a 17-year-old ISIS supporter had almost 4,000 Twitter followers before he was arrested for conspiracy to support ISIS. An Arab-American Islamic preacher named Ahmad Musa Jibril living in Michigan had 38,000 followers before his account was shut down.[12] A study published by the Department of War Studies, King's College London found that,

> Jibril, a U.S. based preacher with Arab roots who is in his early 40s, does not explicitly call to violent jihad, but supports individual foreign fighters and justifies the Syrian conflict in highly emotive terms. He is eloquent, charismatic, and – most importantly – fluent in English.[13]

Not only is there an ever-increasing number of people for the police to watch, but citizens are hesitant to report suspicious activity for fear of being labeled a bigot. Right after the San Bernardino bloodbath one neighbor said she was suspicious of activity at the home of the two murderers but didn't report it to the police because she was fearful of "racial profiling" accusations.[14]

---

[12] (Gorka & Gorka, 2015, p. 1)
[13] (Carter, Maher, & and Neumann, 2014)
[14] (Live Fox News report, December 3, 2015)

Aggressors are looking for soft targets

So why should we be concerned about churches being targeted? Because churches are soft targets. A "soft target" is a facility or event that has little or no protection from attack. Government buildings used to be soft until they hardened their facilities with armed security, metal detectors, and by installing bulletproof glass and locking doors. The aggressors then turned to schools. Not long ago schools were open and inviting. Parents were encouraged to show up unannounced and visit their children's classes. Schools built in the 1970s used open-architecture concepts and no doors on classrooms were in vogue. Those classrooms with doors had windows and no locks. School administrators were more concerned about children being trapped inside and being burned to death in the event of a fire.

According to the National Fire Protection Association (NFPA) the 50 years between 1908 and 1958 there were eight school fires in which ten or more people died, claiming 755 lives. From 1958 to 2015 there have been zero school fires with ten or more deaths.[15] From 755 lives to zero! What happened? We became aware and took measures to prevent unnecessary deaths. Fire retardant material was used in building construction; multiple exits were mandated; fire alarms and sprinkler systems were installed; and firefighters were better trained and equipped. The NFPA also reports that from "2007 to 2011, U.S. fire departments responded to an average of 1,780 structure fires in religious and funeral properties each year."[16] These fires claim only two civilian lives per year, which means one death for every 890 fires.[17] Why are the numbers of fire deaths so low in schools and churches? What were once "soft targets" for fire became

---

[15] (National Fire Protection Association, 2015)
[16] (National Fire Protection Association, 2015)
[17] (National Fire Protection Association, 2015)

hard targets. I'm guessing your church is in compliance with the fire code.

In recent years schools became increasingly harder targets for someone seeking to wreak havoc by mass bloodshed. Schools are no longer "open access" facilities. Resource Safety Officers (RSOs) are commonplace; solid doors with locks and no windows are back; fire drills are accompanied by active-shooter drills; students are encouraged to report any suspicious activities of their fellow students; and police officers have received better training and equipment to deal with the phenomena we call "active shooters."

So, what are the soft targets? Who or what is an easy target for assailants looking to spread terror across America? The answer: any place that has a large gathering of people who are unsuspecting and unprotected. Most churches in America fit this description!

The Merriam-Webster Online Dictionary defines *sanctuary* with three simple, straight forward statements, "a place where someone or something is protected or given shelter; the protection that is provided by a safe place; the room inside a church, synagogue, etc., where religious services are held"[18] There was a time in our country when churches were considered sacred sanctuaries where one would be safe. Today that's simply not the case and the police recognize citizens need to play an active role in their own personal safety. A recent forum of police executives agree the public should know that:

> The prevalence of active shooter incidents has changed police thinking about how community members should respond to a violent offender. Traditionally, police have instructed community members not to resist if

---

[18] (Merriam-Webster, 2015)

they are confronted by a robber, burglar, car-jacker, or other assailant. "Your wallet is not worth your life," police officers say. "Do what the robber tells you and don't fight back."[19]

The traditional response of the public to crime is out the window. Citizens are encouraged not to be passive, but be active because these assassins are of a different mindset. Dialing 911 and waiting for the arrival of the police was the standard trained response to crime. Rather than taking action, we were encouraged to be a "good witness" for the police. As a result we didn't think much about fighting crime. Today's police executives understand that these killers aren't motivated by greed, it's killing that motivates them. Now, like preparing for a fire, we are instructed to prepare in advance. The Police Executive Research Forum reports,

> *Today's police executives understand the active shooter isn't motivated by greed, it's killing that motivates him.*

> [A]ctive shooters are not motivated by rational considerations such as money; their goal is simply to kill. So victims must have a different approach as well. Some police departments have begun to teach community members to think about how they will respond if they ever find themselves in an active-shooter incident.[20]

---

[19] (Police Executive Research Forum, 2014, p. 37)
[20] (Police Executive Research Forum, 2014, p. 37)

Dr. Blair sums up what he believes is the most important message the police can get to citizens:

> The major message that we have for civilians is, "You are not helpless. What you do matters. And what you do can save your own life and the lives of others." Our research found that many times, active-shooter attacks stopped because potential victims took action to stop the shooter directly, or they made it more difficult for the shooter to find targets. In other words, *the actions of civilians can dramatically affect the number of casualties that occur during an attack.* This is a message police can disseminate.[21]

The point is citizens aren't helpless. The response, "I didn't know what to do or say. I was just numb." doesn't need to be our response. Preparation and training are the keys.

Flight or Fight…or Fright?

For years psychologists have taught us that there are two responses to fear: flight or fight. I remember being taught that when faced with danger, and fear kicks in we will either run from danger (flight) or confront danger (fight). West Point psychology professor and former army ranger, Lt. Col. Dave Grossman disagrees that there are but two responses to fear. Grossman says there are at least two additional responses to fear when the threat comes from another human: posturing and submitting.[22]

---

[21] (Police Executive Research Forum, 2014, p. 38)
[22] (Grossman, On Killing, 1996, p. 5)

According to Grossman, soldiers have historically postured by wearing uniforms or armament that made them look larger, displaying weaponry that made them appear stronger, and shooting blasts from muskets and cannons over the enemies' heads intimidating them into surrender.[23] However, at the time an active killing event is happening there is no time for posturing. When an assailant appears with a gun in a room full of people posturing is not a valid response. Further, posturing against those with the mindset that they have come to kill until they are killed will not be an effective tool. Posturing will only work on those who are themselves afraid of being defeated or dying.

Posturing is an attempt to appear stronger, bigger, or in some way superior to one's enemy. When I was in high school my buddy's truck broke down and I decided to borrow some tools, so I headed for a nearby house. Half way across the front yard a large German shepherd lurched from the front porch and bounded toward all 135 pounds of a scrawny 16-year-old boy—me. Wide-eyed and scared my first thought was to run, but I knew I'd never outrun the beast. I also knew I'd be no match in a one-on-one fight. Having a dog of my own, I was hoping this German shepherd would respond to a threatening command. I decided to posture (although I didn't know the technical name for it at the time) by threatening him. Turning to face the charging monster that was now only a few feet from his prey, I looked into the eyes of my foe and yelled with the loudest command voice I could muster, "NO!" The dog stopped in its tracks. I pointed back to the porch and issued a second command, "Get back over there!" To my surprise, and great relief, the now timid canine obeyed while I turned and quickly made it back to the safety of the truck.

---

[23] (Grossman, On Killing, 1996, pp. 5-16)

However, posturing may very well be appropriate prior to an attack, the goal being to prevent an attack. Posturing can be done through the use of: uniformed guards on site; signs that warn an armed team is on duty (e.g. "Warning Armed Safety Response Team on Duty") and other communication that may discourage a person from attempting to carry out an attack at a place of worship.

The second response Grossman adds to the flight-or-fight response is submission. I call this the "fright" response. Fright is the "dumb-and-numb" response. This response is caused by sensory overload. The heart rate is upwards of 175 beats per minute, there's a loss of fine motor skills, and vision and hearing are adversely affected. Grossman calls this "Condition Black," and explains, "As you enter Condition Black, your cognitive processing deteriorates, which is a fancy way of saying you stop thinking."[24]

The first three responses (flight, fight, and posture) are responses to a threat with the goal of removing the threat. The flight response seeks to remove the danger by creating distance between you and the opponent. The fight response seeks to overpower an opponent and win the battle. The posturing response seeks to intimidate the attacker making him believe he cannot prevail. All three of these responses come out of rational thinking. You've heard the expressions "scared stiff," "stage fright," or "paralyzed with fear." The fright response comes out of not thinking. When you can't think you can't act, therefore you submit.

In Roseburg, Oregon, on October 2, 2015 students were in classes at Umpqua Community College when confronted by an armed assailant. Media reports demonstrated that many of the victims were in a state of fright, taking no action to save their own lives. The students took no action, even as the assailant paused to reload and ask questions. They simply submitted to the gunman's demands.

---

[24] (Grossman, On Combat, 2008, pp. 31-44)

The gunman who opened fire at Oregon's Umpqua Community College targeted Christians specifically, according to the father of a wounded student. Before going into spinal surgery, Anastasia Boylan told her father and brother the gunman entered her classroom firing. The professor in the classroom was shot point blank. Others were hit, she told her family.

Everyone in the classroom dropped to the ground.

The gunman, while reloading his handgun, ordered the students to stand up if they were Christians, Boylan told her family.

"And they would stand up and he said, 'Good, because you're a Christian, you're going to see God in just about one second,'" Boylan's father, Stacy, told CNN, relaying her account.

"And then he shot and killed them."[25]

However, one student refused to be a victim and took action—30 year-old Chris Mintz refused to submit. Rather than doing what the gunman ordered, he charged the gunman and was shot seven times for his bravery. Mr. Mintz, an army veteran, survived the shooting and is credited with saving the lives of other students.[26] What was the difference between

---

[25] (Cable News Network, 2015)
[26] (USA Today Network and KGW Staff, 2015)

Mr. Mintz and those who were "dumb and numb"? The difference was conditioning. Because he never entered into Condition Black he was able to think. He understood the assailant wasn't going to quit the killing unless stopped. It was likely his army training helped Mr. Mintz "keep his cool", think, and respond to the threat.

As school children we were conditioned to respond to the sound of a fire alarm. We stopped what we were doing, formed a line, and exited the building while calmly following behind each other as teachers ensured everyone was out. We didn't need to think—we just responded. We responded because we were conditioned to respond to a particular stimulus in a predetermined way. When fire alarms blared throughout the school it startled us, but we quickly identified the sound and responded as conditioned. We had heard the sound before. We had made plans. We responded as planned.

Imagine if there were no fire drills, teachers had never planned, and students were never trained. What do you think the response would be in the event of a real fire? There would be mass chaos. Many school children would simply shut down, submitting to the dangers of a fire, and burn to death.

Over the years countless lives were saved from fire because teachers and students were conditioned to respond to a particular stimulus in a predetermined way. That's the goal of preparing for an active-shooter event. As demonstrated above, police executives recognize the need for citizens to prepare in advance and take action to protect their own lives,

It is important for people to think in advance about how they would respond, because the extremely high stress of an active-shooter incident tends to cause people to freeze. Taking action quickly, and taking the right kinds of actions, are critical to saving your own life and the lives of others.[27]

Therefore, in our new America *preparation* and *training* are necessary fundamentals to have a proper response to an active killer that enters a church facility. Even if church leaders or the congregation decides not to support an armed response, preparation and training are necessary to elicit an acceptable response of flight or fight. Fright is not acceptable, and the only way to avoid a "dumb-and-numb" response is through a conditioned response. Conditioned responses are achieved only through proper preparation and training.

In an interview shortly after the San Bernardino massacre, Detroit police Chief James Craig, said this about armed and trained citizens,

> The reality of the world that I work in and have now for 38 years, is that we respond and react to situations. And if an emergency call for service comes in, shots fired, a massive shooting, terrorist act, we're responding. So in those seconds, those brief seconds, when the first shots are fired, it might be that armed citizen...that law-abiding citizen that's trained.[28]

But isn't there some other means of protection?

On August 28th, 2005, in rural Finnin County, Texas, Fred Cranshaw, unleashed his pent-up fury on members of the Sash Assembly of God Church. Cranshaw, described as an angry neighbor who lived across the street from the

---

[27] (Police Executive Research Forum, 2014, p. 37)
[28] (Live interview with Neil Cavuto, *Your World with Neil Cavuto*, December 4, 2015)

church, had words with members that fateful evening. According to witnesses, Cranshaw complained, "I'm tired of you hymn masters, talking to me and following me every where [sic] I go. I'm going to stop it." One of the members responded, "Sir, I don't know what you're talking about." Cranshaw shot back, "You start off and get smart with me and I'll snap the (expletive) out of you."

Cranshaw departed and returned moments later armed with a pistol. Pastor James Armstrong, 42, and Deacon Eric "Wes" Brown, 61, met Cranshaw in front of the church. Cranshaw shot both men at close range, killing both. He fled on foot and murdered two more (Holly Brown and Ceri Litterio) in his hateful rage. Hours later Cranshaw committed suicide, refusing to give up to police.[29]

The prophet Jeremiah laments with the chilling question, *"Should priest and prophet be killed in the sanctuary of the Lord?"* (Lam. 2:20). Could the murder of Pastor Armstrong and three others have been prevented? We don't know for sure, but if the Sash Church had Safety Response Teams in place there's a good possibility there would not have been as many casualties. In this case the assailant caused a disturbance, he departed, and then returned with a pistol. If a trained, *un*armed Safety Response Team (detailed in chapter 3) addressed Cranshaw initially and called the police, perhaps there would have been no lives lost.

"A wise man is full of strength, and a man of knowledge enhances his might, for by wise guidance you can wage your war, and in abundance of counselors there is victory."
(Proverbs 24:5-6)

---

[29] (News 12 KXII staff reporters, 2005)

What does Scripture say?
Chapter 2

Guards in the sanctuary?! Who would consider such measures? How about Moses, *"There were 8,600, keeping guard over the sanctuary,"* (Num. 3:28). However, just about any case can be made from Scripture, especially when using only a single verse. Throughout the two thousand years of Church history popes, priests, pastors, and professors have all made cases from Scripture, yet often came to different conclusions from the same text. As a pastor and Christian college professor my goal is to present a right view of Scripture.

To be frank, nowhere does the Bible say explicitly, "A local church shall have an armed security team." Neither does the Bible say, "A local church shall *not* have an armed security team." While there are many things the Bible speaks to directly and unequivocally it doesn't specifically address armed security teams in a local church or faith-based organization. So what do we do? We look to biblical principles. The question isn't, "Did Jesus say to protect a local New Testament church with armed guards?" The question is, "What is the overarching witness of Scripture concerning self-defense or defense of another using lethal force?"

Joshua fights with the sword

"Then Amalek came and fought with Israel at Rephidim."
(Exodus 17:8)

It was less than three months since Moses led Israel out of Egypt. Following ten devastating plagues, Israel was finally free and safely across the Red Sea while Egypt's army died in a watery grave. But Egypt's army wasn't the last threat Israel faced. After crossing the Red Sea Israel encountered three life-threatening dilemmas, two dealt with water, one with food. In each incidence the Lord miraculously provided for his people. The Lord cured non-potable water with a stick, provided daily manna from Heaven, and caused water to come from a rock.[30]

After the Lord demonstrated his ability to provide for and sustain his people against the brutal desert elements, Israel rested at Rephidim. Rephidim was the last stop before Mt. Sinai, where they would worship God and receive further instruction from him.

Rephidim means rest or resting place.[31] While at this resting place, Israel is attacked by the Amalekite army. *"Then Amalek came and fought with Israel at Rephidim"* (Exod. 17:8). Israel was at a place of rest when attacked. This was a first for Israel. While living in Egypt as slaves for the last 400 years she fell under their protection. But Egypt wasn't there to protect her anymore. Even in bondage there's a certain amount of security. In Egypt, while not free, they had food, water, and the protection of the Egyptian army. When they chose to follow the Lord they lost all that Egypt provided, exchanging it for what the Lord promised. So it should be no surprise that an attack came.

---

[30] (See Exod. 15:22-27; 16:1-8; 17:1-7)
[31] (Blue Letter Bible, n.d.)

But didn't the Lord promise they wouldn't be attacked? Couldn't he have prevented an attack? No, the Lord never promised they wouldn't be attacked; and yes, he could have prevented it, but didn't. The Lord promised salvation. He promised deliverance. He promised to be with them. The Lord never promised his people protection from the harm sin brings as they journeyed to the Promised Land.

Israel was in a position of vulnerability simply because she followed the Lord's leading. That's when Amalek attacked. The Amalekites were a nomadic people that traveled about attacking and looting nations. The Amalekites had domesticated the camel and used its speed to ambush unsuspecting victims, relieving them of their possessions.[32] Israel should have been easy prey for these Amalekites, who were skilled in warfare.

The Amalekites had learned where Israel was camped and threatened to attack a people unskilled in warfare. What would Israel do? Israel had been slaves, not soldiers. They were brick-makers, not warriors. They were shepherds, not combatants. Word had spread that Israel had left Egypt with a large bounty and no army making them an easy target for Amalek.

So, what did Israel do? Throw her hands up in surrender? Compromise in an attempt to make peace? Turn tail and run? No, she stood and fought. *"So Moses said to Joshua, 'Choose for us men, and go out and fight with Amalek'"* (Exod. 17:9a). *"So* Joshua did as Moses told him [emphasis added], *and fought with Amalek"* (Exod. 17:10a). *"And Joshua overwhelmed Amalek and his people with the sword"* (Exod. 17:13).

Amalek was defeated "with the sword." Why didn't the Lord protect Israel with a miracle? Why didn't the Lord confuse the Amalekites like he would the Syrian army years later? Why? The text doesn't say, but we know this, God

---

[32] (Stuart, 2006, p. 393)

21

used his people to protect themselves with the common weapon of combat: a sword.

David guarding the sheep

"Choose a man for yourselves, and let him come down to me. If he is able to fight with me and kill me.... But if I prevail against him and kill him...."
(1 Samuel 17:8-9)

One of the most famous stories in the Bible is David's defeat of Goliath with a stone from a sling. The sling, like the modern day handgun, was a common handheld weapon used for self-defense, hunting, and close combat.[33] In the hands of a skilled slinger these were deadly weapons.[34]

Israel and the Philistines were at a standstill the Philistines wanted Israel to either send out a champion to fight against their giant or surrender. That was when a young shepherd named David arrived on the scene. And just as he had done previously, Philistine giant Goliath taunts and challenges Israel's army to send a man to fight him. David immediately goes on the offensive. *"David said to the men who stood by him, 'What shall be done for the man who kills this Philistine and takes away the reproach from Israel?'"* (1 Sam. 17:26a). David pulled no punches. But none of Israel's soldiers stepped forward to fight the giant. One of those unwilling soldiers was Eliab, David's brother who responds, *"Why have you come down? And with whom have you left those few sheep in the wilderness? I know your presumption and the evil of your heart, for you have come down to see the battle"* (1 Sam. 17:28b). However, David didn't give in, because he knew he was on the side of right. God's people were

---

[33] (2 Chron. 26:14)
[34] (1 Chron. 12:1-2)

22

being threatened by the arrogant Philistine giant and Israel's king and army weren't willing to fight, but David was. David said to King Saul, *"Let no man's heart fail because of him. Your servant will go and fight with this Philistine"* (1 Sam. 17:32).

David wasn't a soldier he was a shepherd. He'd never been in battle, nor trained in hand-to-hand combat, and he was young. Goliath was a trained and proven warrior. Saul warned him, *"You are not able to go against this Philistine to fight with him, for you are but a youth, and he has been a man of war from his youth"* (1 Sam. 17:33). David responded, *"Your servant used to keep sheep for his father. And when there came a lion, or a bear, and took a lamb from the flock, I went after him and struck him and delivered it out of his mouth. And if he arose against me, I caught him by his beard and struck him and killed him"* (1 Sam. 17:34-35). David had skills to protect his father's sheep from a deadly predator attack and he saw Goliath as the lion or bear; a predator. *"Your servant has struck down both lions and bears, and this uncircumcised Philistine shall be like one of them, for he has defied the armies of the living God"* (1 Sam. 17:36). I wonder if Saul read between the lines. Did he realize David not only compared Goliath to a lion or bear, but he also compared Israel's army to sheep?

David was a shepherd and his job was to protect the flock. He saw Israel's army as sheep that were paralyzed by the threats of a giant predator. Not only did David have the will and the skill he also believed, *"The LORD who delivered me from the paw of the lion and from the paw of the bear will deliver me from the hand of this Philistine"* (1 Sam. 17:37a).

David didn't propose a prayer meeting to decide what to do. David didn't presume if they talked to the Philistines something could be worked out. David knew immediate action needed to be taken. Goliath threatened violence and David proposed to respond with violence. King Saul said, *"Go, and the* LORD *be with you!"* (1 Sam. 17:37b). David did go. *"So David prevailed over the Philistine with a sling and with a stone, and struck the Philistine and killed him,"* (1 Sam. 17:50). Why didn't David attempt to reason with Goliath? Why didn't David try to make peace? Because it was not the time. David's son Solomon would later write, *"For everything there is a season, and a time for every matter under heaven... a time for war, and a time for peace"* (Ecc. 3:1, 8b).

Nehemiah—armed and ready

"The wall of Jerusalem is broken down, and its gates are destroyed by fire."
(Nehemiah 1:3)

Nehemiah led a contingent of Jews to Jerusalem to rebuild the city's walls that were broken down years earlier when Nebuchadnezzar had attacked the city and forced Judah into Babylonian exile. For nearly 150 years the walls lay in ruin. The walls of a city was its protection against attack. A city without walls was a defenseless city. A city without walls was a vulnerable city. A city without walls was at the mercy of any army that wanted to attack. God's people were vulnerable to physical assault. We read, *"As soon as I [Nehemiah] heard these words I sat down and wept and mourned for days, and I continued fasting and praying before the God of heaven"* (Neh. 1:4). Nehemiah understood the implications of an unprotected people in a hostile environment.

Jerusalem needed her walls rebuilt and Nehemiah was called by God to lead in the rebuilding. Nehemiah, although a Jew, was an official in the court of the Persian king Artaxerxes. After securing permission from Artaxerxes, Nehemiah made the trip to Jerusalem and rallied the Jewish people to begin the rebuilding effort. But there were enemies of the Jews that didn't want the walls restored, the Bible records that *"it displeased them greatly that someone had come to seek the welfare of the people of Israel"* (Neh. 2:10b). Imagine that! There are those who don't want God's people to be safe.

Three enemies are named in Nehemiah chapter two: Sanballat, Tobiah, and Geshem. When they heard of Nehemiah's plans they asked, *"What is this thing that you are doing? Are you rebelling against the king?"* (Neh. 2:19b). Nehemiah replied, *"The God of heaven will make us prosper, and we his servants will arise and build, but you have no portion or right or claim in Jerusalem"* (Neh. 2:20). Nehemiah's default response to adversity was prayer and faith.

Prayer and faith. Two foundational tenants of God's people not only in the Old Testament, but in the New as well. Paul writes in Philippians, *"Do not be anxious about anything, but in everything by prayer and supplication with thanksgiving let your requests be made known to God"* (Phil. 4:6). That's what Nehemiah did first—he prayed to God. Second, he expressed faith that God "will make us prosper." Faith is pleasing to God. In fact, *"And without faith it is impossible to please him, for whoever would draw near to God must believe that he exists and that he rewards those who seek him"* (Heb. 11:6).

Prayer and faith. But was that the extent of Nehemiah's defense against his enemies? Was there any more to do? We continue reading that the work began and things were moving quickly. In no time the wall took shape and it caught the eye of their enemies. *"Now when Sanballat heard that we were building the wall, he was angry and greatly enraged, and he jeered at the Jews"* (Neh. 4:1). But these were just words and the work continued. Nehemiah again prayed and reported on the work, *"So we built the wall. And all the wall was joined together to half its height, for the people had a mind to work"* (Neh. 4:6).

The work and success of God's people infuriated their enemies who turned from verbal insults to threats of physical assault. *"And they all plotted together to come and fight against Jerusalem and to cause confusion in it"* (Neh. 4:8). Nehemiah could have either: stopped the work God called him to do; or tried to negotiate with those opposed, insisting that peace was the most important thing. After all, isn't peace more important than some brick and mortar wall? Apparently Nehemiah didn't think so. We read that Nehemiah, *"prayed to our God and set a guard as a protection against them day and night,"* (Neh. 4:9). Nehemiah prayed and set a guard. However, the guard wasn't just a lookout to report if the bad guys were coming, but they were armed citizens, *"I stationed the people by their clans, with their swords, their spears, and their bows"* (Neh. 4:13b). The sword, spear, and bow were common weapons of war and self-defense in that day.

Why were they armed to protect a wall? Because it was more than a wall at stake; it went deeper than that. It was a matter of life and death; the life and death of their families. Nehemiah understood the gravity of the threat. He said, *"Do not be afraid of them. Remember the Lord, who is great and awesome, and fight for your brothers, your sons, your daughters, your wives, and your homes"* (Neh. 4:14b). And so, *"Neither I nor my brothers nor my servants nor the men of the guard who followed me, none of us took off our clothes; each kept his weapon at his right hand"* (Neh. 4:23). The phrase *"at his right hand,"* has also been interpreted *"even when he went for water"* (NIV). The point Nehemiah was making is that they remained armed and ready at all times.

The results were amazing; *"So the wall was finished...in fifty-two days"* (Neh. 6:15). In the end, Nehemiah gave credit to God for their success, *"And when all our enemies heard of it, all the nations around us were afraid and fell greatly in their own esteem, for they perceived that this work had been accomplished with the help of our God"* (Neh. 6:16). It must be noted that while Nehemiah prayed and trusted God he also used armed guards to protect the people. Their enemies knew they were armed and ready.

Elisha commissioned to kill

"Elisha...you shall anoint to be prophet in your place."
(1 Kings 19:16)

Elisha was a man of the cloth. He was a prophet. He was clergy. He wasn't a military leader like Joshua; he wasn't a future king like David; he wasn't even an armed engineer like Nehemiah. He was a spokesman for God. Elisha was called to proclaim the word of God in perilous times. Elisha lived during a season of lawlessness and violence, and it started at the top with Israel's king. King Ahab was second only to his wife Queen Jezebel in wickedness. *"There was none who sold himself to do what was evil in the sight of the Lord like Ahab, whom Jezebel his wife incited"* (1 Kings 21:25). Jezebel's solution for those who dared to defy her was their execution. She executed God's prophets,[35] she sentenced to death an innocent man named Naboth simply because he refused to sell a piece of land her husband, [36] and she put out a contract to kill Elisha's predecessor Elijah. [37] This was the situation in Israel when Elisha was called to be a prophet.

Elijah fled from Jezebel's threat of death and feared his life was over. But the Lord ordered Elijah to anoint three men to special positions: Hazael as Syria's king, Jehu as Israel's king, and Elisha as a prophet to take his place. These three men were commissioned by the Lord to put a violent end to Ahab's evil regime. Hazael would kill Ahab in battle

---

[35] (1 Kgs. 18:13)
[36] (1 Kgs. 21:1-16)
[37] (1 Kgs. 19:2)

and Jehu would execute Jezebel and several other relatives of the royal family.[38]

Hazael, Jehu, and Elisha—two kings and a prophet. Two men of violence, and a man of the cloth. Two men who wouldn't hesitate to kill in order to secure a throne, and a spokesman for God. While there's not much information about Hazael's military background we do know that he was a violent and vile man. He was an official for Ben-Hadad I, king of Syria. Ben-Hadad was terminally ill and Hazael hastened death by smothering the king with a wet towel to secure the throne for himself.[39] Jehu was also a man of violence. He was a military commander in Israel's army and was anointed as king to *"strike down the house of Ahab"* (2 Kgs. 9:7). He personally saw to the killing of several men. So what was Elisha's part? Was the job of this prophet to only pray? No, he too was commissioned to kill. *"And the one who escapes from the sword of Hazael shall Jehu put to death, and the one who escapes from the sword of Jehu shall Elisha put to death"* (1 Kgs. 19:17).

Joshua, David, Nehemiah, and Elisha. Four men of God all commissioned by the Lord to use deadly force in protecting his people. The overarching witness from the Old Testament clearly shows God sanctioned the use of deadly force to protect innocent lives. However, can we use these Old Testament stories after the revelation of the New Testament? Let us read and ponder the Apostle Paul's words concerning exactly this same question. *"Now these things happened to them as an example, but they were written down for our instruction, on whom the end of the ages has come"* (1 Cor. 10:11). But we have more than just Paul's words. We also have a witness from the New Testament.

---

[38] (1 Kgs. 22:29-36; 2 Kgs. 9)
[39] (2 Kgs. 8:15)

Peter carried a sword

"Lord, shall we strike with the sword?"
(Luke 22:49)

Peter was a fisherman called to be an apostle. In fact, Peter (whose name was Simon until Jesus changed it to Peter) and his brother Andrew were the first of the disciples called to follow the Savior. Peter and the others were with Christ for about three years before he was arrested in the Garden of Gethsemane. The garden was a regular retreat for Jesus and the Twelve, so the traitor Judas knew exactly where they were. He left the Passover meal early to alert the Jewish authorities seeking to arrest Christ.

Jesus knew exactly what he was walking into that fateful night. He understood what was to come when he led his disciples to the garden to pray and requested they too watch and pray.[40] But while Jesus prayed and the disciples fell asleep, until awakened by Judas, leading a crowd of soldiers, temple officers, and Jewish elders armed with swords and clubs to arrest the Lord. The ever impulsive Peter sprang into action, ready to defend his Master. In fact, he did defend Jesus, *"Then Simon Peter, having a sword, drew it and struck the high priest's servant and cut off his right ear"* (John 18:10).

This sword (as one scholar notes) might not be much more than a dagger.[41] However, it could also be the popular Roman short sword with its eighteen inch blade. Either way, it begs the question, "What was Peter doing with a sword?" He wasn't expecting Jesus' arrest. Jesus' arrest and crucifixion took the disciples by surprise. Why then was Peter armed? A sword or dagger was a popular weapon for self-defense. In fact, Jesus even told his disciples that didn't have

---

[40] (The record of Jesus' arrest is recorded in all four Gospels: Matt. 26:36-56; Mark 14:32-50; Luke 22:39-53; John 18:1-11)
[41] (Carson, 1991, p. 579)

29

swords to buy one, *"And let the one who has no sword sell his cloak and buy one"* (Luke 22:36). During the three years that Peter followed Christ it was likely commonplace for Peter to carry a sword. Jesus simply responds to Peter's actions with, *"Put the sword back into its sheath"* (John 18:11). Notice that Jesus didn't correct Peter for his initiative, but told him he could have called to his Father for a legion of angels however, his mission was to fulfill Scripture. Neither did Jesus tell Peter to get rid of the sword.

What's the take away? It's likely that Peter, one of Jesus' apostles and closest friends, regularly carried a deadly weapon for self-defense and for three years the Lord never condemned him or told him not to carry it. When Peter did use deadly force in an effort to protect his Master, Jesus simply told him to put the sword back in its sheath.

What did Jesus say?

"Deliver us from evil."
(Matt. 6:13)

Jesus often spoke in parables. The Greek word transliterated as *parable* means to place alongside for comparison. Jesus took what was familiar (e.g. a farmer sowing seed) and placed it alongside what was unfamiliar (e.g. the Kingdom of God). This comparison used the familiar to shed light on the unfamiliar. Jesus did this when he shared this parable, *"When a strong man, fully armed, guards his own palace, his goods are safe. But when one stronger than he attacks him and overcomes him, he takes away his armor in which he trusted and divides his spoil"* (Luke 11:21-22). Even during the famous "Pax Romana" (the peace of Rome)—when Roman soldiers were present to ensure law and order—bearing arms for personal protection was so acceptable and commonplace that Jesus could use it for his parables.

Many Christians point to the Sermon on the Mount to defend a pacifist position. Jesus said, *"Do not resist the one who is evil"* (Matt. 5:39a). The KJV says *"resist not evil"* but the context (as the ESV and almost all new translations indicate) demonstrates Jesus was referring to an evil *person*, not evil itself. Especially since elsewhere in the Bible we are commanded to resist evil. And from the earlier examples of this chapter we see that we are even to take a stand against evil in the form of physical attacks. In the Sermon on the Mount Jesus addressed our response to non-believing individuals who treat believers unfairly. Christ was speaking about those who are dishonest or unjust in their dealings with his followers, he wasn't teaching about how to handle a physical assault.

However, Jesus also said, *"But if anyone slaps you on the right cheek, turn to him the other also"* (Matt. 5:39b). This is a key passage used to promote pacifism, but it is misused by well-meaning people when they suggest that self-defense is wrong. They believe that the "Christian" thing to do is to remain passive while an aggressor physically assaults you. As a young boy this verse caused me considerable guilt when I defended myself against the playground bully. But Jesus wasn't talking about physical assault in the Sermon on the Mount. Rather, he was addressing verbal personal insults.

A slap to the right cheek indicated a backhanded slap to the face as a show of disdain or scorn for another, it wasn't seen as a physical assault. It was regarded as a grossly offensive insult, and is still regarded as a serious insult in the Near East today.[42]

This attack went directly against a person's self-esteem, ego, character, or reputation. In our society we call this libel, verbal assault, or an insulting gesture. It amounts to speaking badly about someone, spreading rumors, or hurting

---

[42] (Furguson, 1988, p. 100)

with cutting words or comments. Jesus was saying don't try to even the score by trading insults with another; even if it means you receive more insults. Both the textual and cultural contexts support the understanding that Jesus' words were referring to a verbal insult, and not a physical attack.

Furthermore, in this section (Matt. 5:38-42) Jesus is teaching about *revenge*, not self-defense. He introduces the section with, *"You have heard that it was said, 'An eye for an eye and a tooth for a tooth'"* (Matt. 5:38). Revenge is an action that takes place after the offense is committed and the threat has passed.

The Greek word translated *resist* means to be set against, to withstand, or to oppose.[43] Jesus, in teaching about retaliating, says we are not to set ourselves against another by trying to even the score. We are not to withstand another by lashing out. We are not to seek revenge. Does this mean it was wrong to oppose the likes of Stalin, Hitler, and Hussein? No, that's not what Jesus meant. Does it mean we may not file charges against someone who burglarizes our home? No, that's not what Jesus meant. Does it mean we cannot defend ourselves during a physical assault? No! That's not what Jesus meant! Then, what did Jesus mean?

Jesus was talking about our everyday relationships with others. Jesus was referring to common relationships we have with our co-workers, peers at school, the store employee, the hairdresser, or the auto mechanic—people we encounter daily who may treat us unfairly. People who are dishonest with us. People who personally wrong us. By saying, *"Do not resist the one who is evil"* Jesus essentially meant, don't retaliate against those who personally wrong you.

A balanced approach is in order.

---

[43] (Biblical Studies Press, L.L.C., 1996-2006)

A Balanced Approach

"Vengeance is mine, I will repay, says the Lord."
(Romans 12:20)

So, what's the take-away from our overview? Are we to be paranoid, gun-toting, vigilantes? Absolutely not. As demonstrated from Scripture, a balanced approach is in order. Above all we are to have faith in God. Faith in God and taking personal responsibility is a balanced approach. This is what Nehemiah did, *"And we prayed to our God and set a guard as a protection against them day and night"* (Neh. 4:9). Nehemiah trusted God and set a guard. Joshua trusted God and wielded a sword. David trusted God and used a sling. When I was a police officer I trusted God and wore my bulletproof vest. I trusted God and carried a nightstick. I trusted God and carried my service pistol. When I drove my young children I trusted God and secured them in a safety seat. At home I trust God and lock my doors. The overarching witness from Scripture about self-defense is that we are to trust God and take responsible action.

Jesus, speaking to believers, said, *"This is my commandment, that you love one another as I have loved you"* (John 15:12). The next explains, *"Greater love has no one than this, that someone lay down his life for his friends"* (John 15:13). Laying down your life is done by intervening on another's behalf. Intervening means standing in the gap. Coming between an aggressor and a victim.

As a husband and father I'm compelled by love to protect my wife and children from harm. Scripture tells me I'm to protect them even if it costs me my life, *"Husbands, love your wives, as Christ loved the church and gave himself up for her"* (Eph. 5:25). The obligation to protect my family doesn't end when we step outside the house. When I'm in public I take that obligation with me. This includes when I'm in church.

33

As a pastor I'm charged to protect the congregation the Lord entrusts to me. Paul, speaking to the elders of the churches in Ephesus charges them to, *"Pay careful attention to yourselves and to all the flock, in which the Holy Spirit has made you overseers, to care for the church of God"* (Acts 20:28). While everyone agrees Paul was speaking primarily to spiritual protection I believe he was also speaking to physical protection. In fact, leading up to that statement Paul was talking specifically about his own physical safety.

A peaceable people? Yes, that should be a mark of any local New Testament church. We should, as Paul exhorts, *"live peaceably with all."* But we can only do that if it is possible for us to do so. Here's the whole verse, *"If possible, so far as it depends on you, live peaceably with all"* (Rom. 12:18). When an aggressor wielding a gun walks into a church it is not possible to live in peace.

Organizing a Safety Response Team
Chapter 3

The New Life Incident

On Sunday, December 9, 2007, Carl Chinn, a security team volunteer for New Life Church in Colorado Springs, CO, caught the news before going to church that morning. Hours earlier there was a shooting at Youth With a Mission, 77 miles north of Colorado Springs. Two young people were murdered, and the killer was still on the loose. Chinn gathered the little information available and alerted his team to be extra vigilant that day.

The New Life Church is a large church with several buildings and a campus encompassing thirty acres. Two uniformed Colorado Springs police officers were placed outside and another one was inside the main building. They were hired for extra security. The church services went off without a hitch and by one o'clock things were winding down. The uniformed police officers departed just after one, as per their contract. Several people remained in the buildings for other meetings and events.

One of the security team members radioed there was smoke in the front of one of the entrances. A short time later Chinn heard gunshots that sounded like they were coming from the main entrance. Believing he was the only armed security team member available, Chinn ran towards the sound of the shots. As he entered the long hallway from the staircase he saw a man with a semi-automatic military type rifle coming into the lobby. Unknown to him at the time, the assailant had just murdered two young people in the parking lot. Chinn was a hundred yards from the threat. Armed with a .32 caliber pistol, he closed the distance and found cover behind a large pillar, which was only a few yards away from the assailant.

Chinn knew the gunman was coming his way and anticipated a clear shot as he waited for the assailant to appear from the other side of a pillar. But as he worked to stay focused on the aggressor, Chinn had to contend with two other people. The first was a would-be-hero. He showed up at Chinn's side and wanted to take on the aggressor single-handedly. The stranger stepped out into the open only to draw rifle fire. Although that helped to curtail the would-be-hero's eagerness, he remained a distraction as he kept trying to tell Chinn what to do. It was then that Chinn noticed the second person. A boy crouched behind a counter. Stepping from cover, Chinn got the boy to come to him and then safely exit the building.

As the boy was leaving, Chinn spotted another member of his team positioned across the hallway where Chinn believed the gunman was standing. Jeanne Assam, a former police officer who had recently volunteered to be part of the security team, said something Chinn couldn't make out, "I heard her yell something with authority and knew I was about to see her kill or be killed."[44] Assam opened fire on the assailant with her 9mm pistol, bringing the deadly assault to an end.

Recalling that day, Mr. Chinn writes, "The way the aggressor was quickly and effectively stopped by an intentionally developed church security team set a precedent in

---

[44] (Chinn, Evil Invades Sancuary, 2012, p. 105)

church security culture."[45] For a more detailed description of the event see *Evil Invades Sanctuary* by Carl Chinn.

The organization of a team or teams to protect church members, guests, and staff begins with the purpose or goal of the team(s). Physical peril can come in the form of an armed aggressor, an unarmed aggressor, or a medical emergency either associated or not associated with a physical attack. To effectively respond to any of these threats I suggest the formation of three types of emergency response teams to protect those who attend or work at a house of worship: An **armed** Safety Response Team, an **unarmed** Safety Response Team, and a **medical** Safety Response Team.

The name "Safety Response Team" defines the general purpose of the teams. *The purpose of a Safety Response Team is to provide a team response to an unsafe situation in order to render that situation safe.* Each team member must keep in mind the purpose of the team.

> *The purpose of a Safety Response Team is to provide a team response to an unsafe situation in order to render that situation safe.*

Once the situation is rendered safe then the team's goal changes to maintaining that safety. While the focus of this book is an armed response to armed aggression, it is necessary to mention the other two teams and provide a basic overview of their functions. Carl Chinn provides a more detailed review of supplemental teams and the functions of other support personnel including incident commanders in *Evil Invades Sanctuary*.

Generally speaking, each team is a separate unit and operates separately from the other teams. However, even as distinct teams performing different functions and operating at different times, the teams act in support of each other.

---

[45] (Chinn, Evil Invades Sancuary, 2012, p. 95)

Unarmed Safety Response Team

The purpose of an **unarmed** Safety Response Team (SRT) is to take control of an unarmed aggressor before that aggressor is able to harm any innocent person or disrupt a service. Control is asserted in order to prevent harm to all persons, including the aggressor. Once the aggressor is under control and the situation deescalated, the aggressor is released, escorted from the property, or detained for the police. Disturbances in churches or faith-based organizations are common. Aggressors may include any of the following: disgruntled church members; ex- or estranged spouses; boyfriends; girlfriends; people with mental or spiritual issues that are bent on threatening others, disrupting services, or simply drawing attention to themselves. The key here is unarmed. Unarmed means neither the team nor the disrupter/assailant possess a deadly weapon.

A deadly weapon is any weapon or object that is designed, made, or adapted to inflict serious bodily injury or death. A deadly weapon that is *not* on its face a weapon, but is adapted to inflict serious bodily injury or death include items such as a baseball bat, screw driver, or other object capable of causing blunt trauma, a puncture wound, or other type of serious injury. If a deadly weapon is displayed the *armed* SRT is the proper team to respond.

A knife is a deadly weapon. When I attended the police academy one of the cadets asked our police baton (nightstick) instructor if we were going to be taught "knife take-away" tactics. The instructor responded, "We issue you a 'knife take-away' tactic, it's called a .357 [handgun]." The point being even police officers, to the surprise of many, are not routinely trained to disarm a knife-wielding assailant. Police officers are trained that a person with a knife can cover 21 feet in about two seconds; officers need to be ready and able to shoot quickly in response to a knife-wielding assailant. The principle is this: deadly force must be met with deadly force. In the event an aggressor is armed with a knife he becomes the responsibility of the armed SRT.

An unarmed SRT takes control of a suspect by verbal commands and, if necessary, by using physical force to gain and maintain control.

> *Deadly force must be met with deadly force.*

Members of an unarmed SRT should exhibit the ability to speak calmly in an attempt to deescalate an incident by talking to and removing the aggressor from the sanctuary or separating the aggressor from the person(s) with whom he is upset. In addition members of an unarmed SRT should be physically fit and trained in both verbal and physical control compliance techniques.

While restraint and discretion are in order when dealing with aggressors, unarmed SRT members need to understand and accept the fact that anyone threatening the safety of another must be stopped before things get out of hand. Aggressors sometimes target churches because they believe church people will simply "rollover" and comply with whatever they are told. Unfortunately there is some validity to this belief. Therefore, while a Christian witness needs to be maintained, those responding to the threat need to maintain control in order to ensure safety. While SRT members strive to honor God in their actions, no one has the right to disrupt a worship service or event by causing a disturbance or drawing attention to himself.

What if the person is only being disruptive and destroying property, but not threatening harm to individuals? That will depend on a church's policy or guidelines. One church policy states,

> It is not the policy of the [church's name] to intervene with the **destruction** of the Lord's property with physical intervention. The local law enforcement should be requested for

this assistance. Physical **intervention** should only be applied as necessary to mitigate injury or death to another individual.[46]

If a church body or its leaders decides physical force will only be used to protect people from physical harm that is their choice. However, before implementing such a strict policy a church should consider possible situations. While not using force to protect property may sound noble, in reality it may be neither noble nor wise. I recommend a policy statement that isn't too restrictive. With the above policy in place if someone came into a church and started ripping paintings and decorations off the walls, spray-painting the sanctuary, or breaking windows, any attempt by a member to stop the vandals would be a violation of church policy and could be used against the church and/or the member in a civil lawsuit. Some churches, in an effort to do the right thing, err by making policies or guidelines too restrictive. Using nearly the same language the above policy can be revised to read:

> It is the policy of the [church's name] to *refrain from intervening in the destruction of the Lord's property by* physical intervention. The local law enforcement should be requested for this assistance. Physical **intervention** should only be applied as necessary to mitigate injury or death to another individual, *or in extreme cases of destruction of the Lord's property.*

Adding the word "refrain" and permitting intervention in "extreme cases" allows for discretion and better protects the church and its members from liability while holding to the church's values. Remember policies or guidelines aren't

---

[46] The church name had been deleted.

constitutions or bylaws. Policies and guidelines are designed to help church leaders, staff, and members understand the church's position, the desired outcome, and a suggested course of action under normal or anticipated situations. It's also a good idea to have a statement at the beginning of each policy or guideline that makes it clear that the policy or guideline isn't a "rule" that must never be violated. Here's an example of an opening statement,

> The policies [or guidelines] of this church reflect our values and are understood to be in place as a guide for church leaders and members. We understand every situation cannot be anticipated, hence no policy is intended to be so restrictive as to override the use of common sense or wise discretion.

Medical Safety Response Team

The purpose of a **medical** Safety Response Team (SRT) is to render emergency lifesaving first aid in an effort to sustain life until emergency medical technicians (EMTs) or other medical health professionals arrive. A medical SRT is not to be confused with persons rendering minor first aid for non-life threatening medical emergencies.

A medical SRT should be led by at least one medical professional (i.e. EMT, nurse, or medical doctor). This team is trained to respond to common life threatening medical emergencies such as heart attacks, strokes, seizures, and choking incidents as well as rendering immediate first aid to severe trauma caused by gunshot or stab wounds. For severe trauma cases, the idea is to stop the bleeding and give emotional support until emergency medical personal arrive on scene.

Every church should consider purchasing blood-clotting bandages and tourniquets. The application of these in

41

emergency situations can be taught with a minimal amount of training thereby providing you with a large support team of prepared helpers in the event of mass causalities where several victims may need quick medical attention.

In June 2015 Idaho Falls, Idaho, police officers and Bonneville County deputies responded to a domestic violence call involving Ricky Mosely, 31, who was reported to have a gun. A short time later Mosely was located and threatened the officers, Mosely was shot five times. Immediately after the suspect was down and no longer posing a threat, the very officers that shot him administered first aid, using blood-clotting bandages. The officers' quick actions are credited with saving the suspect's life.

Armed Safety Response Team

The purpose of an **armed** Safety Response Team (SRT) is to quickly neutralize an armed aggressor before that aggressor is able to harm any innocent person. The key to this SRT is speed and efficiency. Response to an armed assailant must be immediate and effective. To neutralize a threat is to eliminate it. An armed aggressor who enters a church brandishing a deadly weapon must be promptly neutralized. This is a life or death situation. The aggressor made the decision to enter the premises to either kill or threaten to kill. It is not the duty of the SRT members to make a determination of the aggressor's intention; it is the team's duty to stop the aggressor. When the assailant made the decision to threaten lives with a deadly weapon he gave up any expectation for his own personal safety.

The emphasis on speed is crucial. An armed aggressor with only a minimal amount of training can easily shoot a semi-automatic pistol 30 to 50 times at aimed targets in a matter of seconds. The most common AR-15 rifle magazine holds 30 rounds, but 60 round magazines are also readily available. Modern firearms enable an assailant armed with either a handgun and/or rifle to quickly maim or kill many people in a short amount of time. Therefore, SRT members must respond and act quickly. What is amazing about mass shootings is that not more people are shot.

Team Members

Selecting team members for an armed SRT is not to be taken lightly. Too often I hear things like, "John likes to hunt, put him on the team," or "Tom has a concealed carry license, he's qualified," or even, "Bill knows a lot about guns, he'd be great!" It must be clear that knowledge of firearms or even skill in shooting firearms isn't enough to qualify a person for an armed SRT. In fact, these don't even top the list. Most anyone can become familiar and trained in the use of firearms. In fact, I found through my private shooting academy and law enforcement experience that it's easier to teach firearms safety, shooting skills, and tactics to someone who has never shot before.

While I was the sergeant in charge of firearms and tactics training for the San Antonio Police Department I discovered that cadets with no shooting experience would often end up being the top shooters by the end of training. In the pre-academy briefing I'd advise cadets that if they had little to no knowledge of firearms not to spend their weekends with "Uncle Bubba" teaching them how to shoot. It's easier to teach a pup new tricks than to break the bad habits of an old dog.

When selecting team members look for the same qualifications the Lord looks for—namely character. When God's people wanted to know what the Lord required the prophet Micah responded *"the Lord has told you what is good, and this is what he requires of you: to do what is right, to love mercy, and to walk humbly with your God"* (Micah 6:8, NLT). The Lord requires three things: do what is right; love mercy; and walk humbly. So don't start with who knows the difference between a gas, blowback, or recoil operating system or who can hit the bull's eye, off-hand, at fifty yards with a .38 Chief's Special. Start with character.

Character

The first requirement is to do what is right. In Micah 6:8, the NIV says to "act justly." When the smoke clears (perhaps literally) you will want to look back knowing that what you did was right. You acted justly. You didn't take the law into your own hands, but responded properly. What comes to mind is the aggressor's wellbeing. "Am I being fair to the assailant?" While that's a legitimate question, that's not the main concern. The main question is, "Am I being fair to those I'm protecting?" The aggressor is the one who's breaking the rules. The aggressor is the one who's threatening lives. The aggressor is the one who's forcing your hand. Select people for the team who are both willing and capable to make the tough decisions in the heat of battle. I will detail more of this in a later chapter.

Second, team members must love mercy or kindness. The Bible says to love our enemies, but it doesn't say to let them kill the sheep. Mercy must be shown to the protected, not the predator. Would it be showing mercy if you had the ability to stop an assailant by shooting him but didn't and rather chose to stand by and allow him to gun down church members one by one? No, of course it wouldn't be showing mercy. It may be showing cowardice, fear, shock, or panic. But allowing killing to take place when someone has the ability and the authority to stop it isn't merciful. In Ezekiel the Lord rebuked the priests, whom he referred to as shepherds, for allowing the people (the sheep) to become prey for wild animals, *"As I live, declares the Lord GOD, surely because my sheep have become a prey, and my sheep have become food for all the wild beasts, since there was no shepherd...Behold, I am against the shepherds,"* (Eze. 34:8-10).

Thirdly, team members must be humble. Humility is exemplified in a willingness to learn and take direction from others. Don't even consider a person who is a "know-it-all." During classroom, live-fire, or reality-based scenario training members must be willing to learn and make adjustments. There's no room for bullheadedness on the team. Furthermore, effective training for the trainers is vital.

If an aggressor is actively killing or threatening to kill, then each team member must respond as trained. Responding out of stubbornness may get people needlessly injured or killed. In any given situation any member of the team may become the team's leader, hence it's imperative that each member be willing to follow the others. Active killing situations are dynamic and adjustments must be made during the course of an event. There's simply no room for a "know-it-all" on an armed SRT—or any SRT for that matter. It's better to run short of personnel than have someone that shouldn't be on the team.

In addition to the three spiritual qualifications of doing what is right, loving mercy, and walking humbly there is one more critical spiritual qualification to consider. Is the person a believer? Has he or she professed faith in Jesus Christ alone for salvation? Just because someone is a longstanding church member or longtime volunteer for a faith-based organization doesn't mean that person has placed their faith in Christ alone for salvation. In fact, many people base their salvation on their good works, church membership, or some other claim of self-righteousness. If someone is going to be asked to stand in harm's way and fill in the gap between an assailant and innocent people, then find out where they stand with the Lord.

Salvation is in Christ alone by faith alone as the apostle Paul writes, *"For by grace you have been saved through faith. And this is not your own doing; it is the gift of God, not a result of works, so that no one may boast,"* (Eph. 2:8-9). A good idea is to have team members share their testimony

45

with the others. Listen carefully for the time when they put their faith in Christ. Not when they started attending church, became a member, began charity work, or was baptized.

Confidentiality is also necessary. Due to the nature of providing protection it will be necessary for team members to be informed of potential problems within the congregation. Team members need to know about any threats between family members, against the pastor or staff, disgruntled members, or others that may pose a threat. This doesn't mean every little spark of discord needs to be reported or treated as a lethal threat! But, situations where deep hatred lies or in which people just won't let things go need to be reported to the team. This means team members need to be trusted to keep their eyes open and mouths shut about the information that is shared with them.

Physical Consideration

Although you're not staffing a SWAT team, physical qualifications should be considered when choosing team members. Everyone has different physical abilities and limitations; keep in mind these naturally diminish over time. Therefore, be aware of and work with the capabilities and limitations of team members. Even a person confined to a wheel chair can be a contributing team member. While understanding the obvious mobility limitations, a person in a wheelchair would have an element of surprise that an aggressor may overlook. Also, it's important for every team member to know their limitations and not to attempt things beyond their own abilities.

Criminal Background and Mental Issues

Criminal background checks should also be considered. Although God forgives our sin in Jesus, the government doesn't. A person may be a potentially great team member, but a convicted felon and cannot legally possess a firearm. Accepting a felon on the team would put the church in a precarious position. Be careful when selecting people to be a member of an armed SRT.

Also, mental health issues need to be addressed. Those under a doctor's care or taking medication for mental health should have written permission from a doctor that they are mentally fit to serve on an armed SRT.

Finding out if someone has a criminal background or mental illness can be difficult. Unless personally aware of everyone's background and mental health (as may be the case in smaller churches) it's best to design an application form asking pointed questions. While a concealed carry license alone doesn't qualify someone for the team, by requiring a concealed carry license, the state does the criminal background check for you.

Aggressor profile

Finally, who are these aggressors that choose to wreak mayhem by indiscriminately killing mass numbers of people gathered at public places? The Federal Bureau of Investigation (FBI) tracks and publishes reports on "active-shooter" incidents. The FBI defines an active shooter as "an individual actively engaged in killing or attempting to kill people in a confined and populated area, typically through the use of firearms."[47] This definition accurately defines whom a church may face—"an individual actively engaged in killing." The term "active shooter" is somewhat of a mis-

---

[47] (Federal Bureau of Investigation, Critical Incident Response Group, n.d.)

nomer. The FBI's own definition supports a better term: "active killer." In this book the terms aggressor, assailant, active shooter, or active killer carry the same meaning and are used interchangeably. Further, since most active shooters are males I'll use the masculine term for the ease of reading when referring to these assailants. But keep in mind, one of the assailants in the San Bernardino incident was a female. These killers aren't limited by gender.

A 2014 study concluded that active killers fit no particular profile other than the vast majority were male. Here are some of their findings: 94% were male from various racial and ethnic backgrounds and ranging in age from 13 to 88 years old; in the majority (55%) of the attacks the aggressor had a prior connection to those he attacked; most attacks were carried out with a handgun (59%), followed by a rifle (26%), and then a shotgun (8%), the rest were unknown to the researchers.[48]

So, the active killer will likely be a male, using a handgun, on those to whom he has some connection. This supports the need for the SRTs (both the armed and unarmed) to be made aware of disgruntled members or members in volatile relationships. For a couple of days prior to the San Bernardino massacre a neighbor noticed several people coming and going. She suspected something was going on and thought about reporting it to authorities but didn't, saying, "I didn't want to racially profile."[49] Perhaps if her suspicions were reported to the authorities the attack would have been prevented. As was pointed out in the New Life incident, intelligence gathering is critical to the safety of the congregation and guests at local houses of worship.

Spiritual Warfare

---

[48] (Federal Bureau of Investigation, Critical Incident Response Group, n.d.)
[49] (Source: Live Fox News report from scene, December 3, 2015)

Although preparing for physical battle, keep in mind the real battle is a spiritual one. Paul writes, *"For we do not wrestle against flesh and blood, but against the rulers, against the authorities, against the cosmic powers over this present darkness, against the spiritual forces of evil in the heavenly places,"* (Eph. 6:12). However, that spiritual battle often manifests itself physically—in *flesh and blood.*

The remainder of this book seeks to help stop the real physical threat to those who gather weekly to worship God. Those who pose a threat may be motivated by hate, spiritual forces of evil, jealousy, anger, or they may be under the influence of drugs, alcohol, or some mental illness. This book isn't about diagnosing, identifying, treating, helping, explaining, accusing, condemning, or excusing the actions of a killer. This book is about effectively and immediately stopping the killing. The other pursuits can be addressed by someone more qualified.

Training—for reality
Chapter 4

The Newhall Shooting

Police learned the hard way that responding during a gunfight is a direct result of training and preparation. In the spring of 1970, two ex-convicts, Jack Twining and Bobby Davis, were traveling through southern California intent on engaging in their own mini crime wave. The ex-cons met and befriended one another in prison; both were released less than a year earlier. The duo planned to rob an armored truck delivering cash to the Santa Anita Racetrack. To pull off the robbery they planned to steal dynamite from a construction site near the city of Newhall, and on the night of April 5, 1970, the felons began to execute their plan. Davis drove their red Pontiac coupe northbound on the Golden State Highway. North of Newhall, they pulled onto the shoulder and stopped near the construction site. Davis waited in the car while Twining went in search of the explosives.

Sitting alone in the Pontiac, Davis became nervous about appearing conspicuous, he made a quick U-turn, and while crossing the median to the southbound lane he nearly hit another car. The car stopped and the couple inside jotted down the Pontiac's license plate number and then pulled up alongside the Pontiac to confront Davis. However, when they approached Davis he pointed a .38 caliber revolver at the driver. The frightened couple sped off and called the police to report the incident.

A short time later, California Highway Patrol (CHP) troopers Roger Gore and Walt Frago spotted the Pontiac traveling southbound. Exiting at Newhall, the red coupe pulled into a parking lot shared by J's Restaurant and a Standard gas station. It was here that the troopers planned to contact the suspect.

There was only supposed to be one suspect, but when

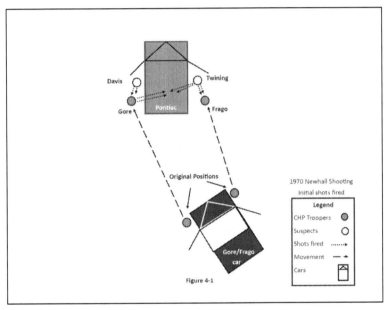

Figure 4-1

Gore and Frago stopped the Pontiac they saw a second man in the passenger seat. Davis stopped the car before pulling all the way into the parking lot, forcing Gore to stop the CHP cruiser at an angle about 20 feet behind the suspects' vehicle. The cruiser's angle provided cover for Gore behind the front left fender, but left the passenger side of the car exposed to the suspects' vehicle (see figure 4-1). Frago exited the passenger side of the patrol car, shotgun held at port-arms (the shotgun held in front of the body with muzzle pointed up and to the left, not towards the threat). Frago had not chambered a round in the shotgun. At that time, CHP had a policy requiring a tape seal over the forend on a shotgun. Chambering a round would break the seal, and any trooper breaking a seal was required to provide a written report to the patrol sergeant detailing why a round was chambered. The intent of this policy was to discourage officers from using their shotguns. It was an effective policy.

It was 11:54 pm when Gore and Frago stopped the Pontiac. From his position behind the left fender, Gore drew his revolver and pointed it at the suspects while he ordered them to exit the car. Davis finally complied after a number of commands. Davis stepped from the driver's seat and stood next to the Pontiac. Ignoring the orders, Twining remained in the passenger seat. Both officers approached the suspect vehicle. While holding Davis at gunpoint, Gore ordered him to spread his legs and place his hands on top of the car. Davis followed his instructions.

While Gore was dealing with Davis, Frago focused his attention on Twining and approached the passenger's side of the Pontiac. Now holding the shotgun only with his

right hand, Frago reached for the passenger door handle with his left hand. Twining suddenly burst from the car and shot Frago twice in the upper torso with a .357 magnum revolver, killing the officer as he dropped to the pavement. Gore's attention immediately went from Davis to Twining. The two exchanged gunfire, but neither hit his target. Davis then pulled his .38 caliber revolver from his waistband (the one he used earlier to threaten the driver of the southbound vehicle) and shot Gore twice in the chest, killing him instantly. It was now 11:55 pm, less than one minute after the stop.

Just one moment later, at 11:56 pm, a second CHP cruiser with troopers James Pence and George Alleyn arrived and parked on the left side of Gore and Frago's patrol car (see figure 4-2). Before the second patrol car came to a

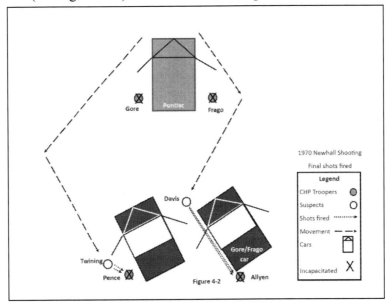

Figure 4-2

stop it started taking gunfire from Davis and Twining who had moved to the front of their Pontiac and were using it for cover. Alleyn exited the passenger's side of the patrol vehicle, shotgun in hand, and moved to the rear of Gore and Frago's car for cover. Pence bailed out of the driver's seat and took a position of cover behind the front left fender of his cruiser. Alleyn, still taking shots from the assailants, racked the shotgun twice, sending an unspent .12 gauge shell to the ground.

Pence and Alleyn began exchanging gunfire with Davis and Twining. Alleyn ran his shotgun dry and Davis, now armed with a shotgun of his own, advanced on Alleyn closing the distance. Alleyn responded shooting his revolver at Davis. Alleyn's shots went awry as Davis hit his mark. Meanwhile, Pence emptied his six-shot service revolver and was reloading when Twining rushed him. Twining executed Pence before he could finish reloading. It was now 11:58, four minutes after the initial stop—four officers lay dead.

During the mayhem a civilian witness, Gary Kness, came upon the shooting after Officers Pence and Alleyn were already engaged in the gunfight. Mr. Kness ran to assist the officers and was able to pick up Alleyn's revolver that lay next to his body and shoot at Davis. Davis received a minor non-life threatening wound from a bullet that likely ricocheted off the Pontiac. The second time Mr. Kness pulled the trigger the hammer fell on a spent cartridge. Out of ammunition and hearing sirens from other officers nearing the scene, Mr. Kness retreated to safety.

After murdering Pence and Alleyn, Davis and Twining returned to their car and fled. A short distance later they abandoned the car and retreated on foot. Twining, who had vowed never to return to prison, committed suicide. Davis was apprehended and sentenced to death, his sentence was later reduced to life in prison.[50] In 2009, Davis died behind bars of an apparent suicide. For an excellent detailed analysis of the shooting see *Newhall Shooting, A Tactical Analysis* by Mike Wood.

The tragic murder of four police officers in what became known as the "Newhall Incident" rocked the law enforcement community. For the first time in American history four law enforcement officers were slain in one incident. All four had been with the CHP for less than two years. Troopers Gore and Frago were 23; troopers Pence and Alleyn were 24. All were husbands and fathers. Although none of the officers were rookies, they were all rather new to the job, not long out of training. What went wrong? How could two ex-convicts outgun four trained professional police officers? The Newhall shooting caused police administrators to take a closer look at police training and their practices for preparing officers to fight with their guns.

Reality Based Training

The importance of training and preparation cannot be overstated. Professional athletes know the importance of proper preparation. The Golden State Warriors' guard Stephen Curry is one of National Basketball Association's (NBA) best jump-shooters. Curry led the Warriors to win the 2015 NBA World Championship and to start the next season with a best ever start for any team in the league's history. Curry's God-given abilities to perform under the stress of playing in high-pressure games before thousands of fans and millions of TV viewers are fine-tuned through training and preparing before game time.

In addition to his regular workout routine and team practices, Curry prepares physically and mentally on the

---

[50] (Wood, 2013)

court for 75 minutes prior to each game. In his pre-game routine, Curry practices jump shots from different places on the court while visualizing his opponent guarding him. Here's how a writer from the *New York Post* reported Curry's pre-game regimen at Brooklyn's Barclays Center, where Curry scored 11 of his 28 points in the third quarter to lead the Warriors to a victory over the Nets.

> Barclays Center turned into Steph World on Sunday night. And it was beautiful to see. This all started 75 minutes before the game. There was Stephen Curry going through his artistic pregame shooting routine, hitting jumpers from every angle on every spot on the floor as his side of the court was stuffed with onlookers.
>
> Curry was simply imagining what was to come later. When it was real, he did the exact same thing at the end of the third quarter as the guard exploded for 11 of the Warriors' final 13 points of the quarter.[51]

Curry knows that training and preparation aren't only for physical conditioning—it's also for mental conditioning. In the best way he can, Curry mimics real-life situations while making his shots. Curry understands his performance in a real game is directly related to this pre-game simulation. The result? Curry is the best in the game, and his team keeps on winning.

The Newhall shooting was the catalyst that transformed police training into what is now known as *Reality Based Training* (RBT). Reality Based Training seeks to mimic the real-life situations police officers face in the

---

[51] (Kernan, 2015)

course of their daily work. This is exactly what Stephen Curry does before each game. However, even during the most intense contest the worst thing Curry will ever face is losing a basketball game. A gunfight is different. Bill Jordan, retired Assistant Chief Patrol Inspector of the Border Patrol, titled his classic 1965 book about gunfights, *No Second Place Winner*. While the losers of a basketball game will live to play another game, a loser in a gunfight may not live to see another day. Jordan's book, directed at law enforcement, teaches officers how to win a gunfight, not how to come in second.

There are two basic aspects to prepare for a gunfight, learning *how* to shoot and learning *when* to shoot. This means training must include both practical shooting techniques and real-life scenarios. Director of Training at Armiger Police Training Institute, Kenneth Murray, put it this way, "When learning how to fight with a pistol or a rifle, teaching a man *how to shoot* is vastly easier than teaching him *how to think* his way through a gunfight."[52]

> *"When learning how to fight with a pistol or a rifle, teaching a man* how to shoot *is vastly easier than teaching him* how to think *his way through a gunfight."*— Kenneth Murray

The proliferation of public shootings has caused ministers and church leaders to at least think about their church's response to an active killer invading the sanctuary. Some remain in denial while I've heard other pastors say things like, "I've got a couple guys in my church who have their concealed carry permits. They'll take care of it."

The Newhall shooting taught us that even trained law enforcement professionals don't automatically hit what they're aiming at in a real combat situation. The four officers

---

[52] (Murray K. R., 2004, p. 14)

obviously passed all their department's required marksmanship training for revolvers and shotguns, but they were unprepared for using those skills during real-life engagement. These four officers in the Newhall shooting fired a total of 11 rounds from their revolvers with zero hits. Frago never got a shot off and Alleyn missed with his shotgun. A good question to ask is: Has the use of RBT in police training since 1970 helped officers achieve a better hit ratio?

For years researchers found that the hit ratio for officer involved shootings was a miserable 15-25%. This suggests that under the pressure of real gunfire performance plummets.[53] That means that 75-85% of the time officers miss. However, Dr. Bill Lewinski, executive director of the Force Science Research Center at Minnesota State University-Mankato reports that a 2005 study by Firearms Trainer Tom Aveni shows actual hits for some agencies to be better. In one large, metropolitan agency the hit rate was 64% for daytime shootings and 45% for shootings occurring in low light (which includes inside lighting conditions). The study also revealed that hit counts went down when the number of shots fired went up and when more officers were involved in the shooting. One agency reported,

> [W]hen only one officer fired during an encounter, the average hit ratio was 51 percent. When an additional officer got involved in shooting, hits dropped dramatically, to 23 percent. With more than 2 officers shooting, the average hit ratio was only 9 percent.[54]

According to Aveni's research the numbers are better than originally thought. However, here's the reality: police officers involved in inside shootings still only have a hit rate of

---

[53] (Lewinski, PoliceOne.com, 2005)
[54] (Lewinski, PoliceOne.com, 2005)

less than 50% in the best trained agencies, and this hit rate drops dramatically when more officers are involved. These are trained police officers. What hit ratio do you think civilians with little or no training will have? What or who will those bullets hit? This is why training is so critical.

While law enforcement officers only have about a 50% hit rate, the other 50% that miss their intended target rarely hit innocent victims—why? Training and preparation. One of the four basic firearms safety rules is to be aware of the target and beyond.[55]

Reality Based Training helps train and prepare officers for real-life gunfights. The guns carried by an armed Safety Response Team are just as deadly as those carried by the police. Therefore, it is necessary for any armed Safety Response Team to engage in scenario training that mimics real-life incidents.

The Mind Matters

Most police departments require officers to qualify with their handguns annually (and in some agencies more often). The typical course-of-fire consists of shooting at paper targets from various distances generally ranging from 3 to 25 yards. At each stage officers are told the number of rounds to shoot, the time limit, and if they must perform a reload or clear a malfunction. In the days before the Newhall Incident, that was about it. If officers could demonstrate the ability to punch a predetermined number of holes in a paper target that wasn't moving or shooting back, then they were good to go. And go they did. Right into gunfights that ended with officers missing their targets more often than hitting them, or even worse being killed. Clearly the officers were physically prepared; on the gun range they demonstrated the

---

[55] (The four basic rules are covered in chapter six, Firearms Basics)

skill to shoot and hit what they were shooting. But that's only half the battle. The other half is between the ears—mental preparation. Bill Jordan writes, "Almost invariably a man, provided he does not have too much time to think, will automatically do what he has been trained to do. Again provided that his training has been thorough and intensive."[56]

Therefore, Reality Based Training must begin with an understanding of basic physiological conditions that may affect performance during a real-fire scenario. Just as athletes mentally prepare before a game, so too must those who choose to carry a gun to protect others prepare for genuine threats. Furthermore, athletes also understand that they must mentally stay in the game. Anyone who watches sporting events understands this important concept. Not staying mentally focused is why teams blow big leads. As the late Yogi Berra quipped, "Baseball is 90% mental, the other half physical." While we chuckle, the Hall of Fame player and long-time coach made his point. Mental preparation is key to being a winner.

There are different "mental conditions" we can be in at any one time. Those who've had the pleasures of raising children know the difference between hearing and listening. When my children were in their teens I'd often give them instructions, to which they acknowledged with a nod of the head and maybe even a "Yes, sir." But, in reality they were oblivious to what I said. They heard, but they weren't aware. In the *Basic Personal Protection in the Home Course* the National Rifle Association (NRA) refers to these conditions as *levels of awareness*. The NRA teaches four basic levels:

- Unaware
- Aware
- Alert

---

[56] (Jordan, 1965, p. 105)

- Alarm[57]

In the *unaware* level we are unconscious of our surroundings. This occurs when we are involved in an activity that occupies our mind. It doesn't take much to occupy the mind. It could be watching TV, talking, reading, etc. For my teenagers it was whatever they were doing other than paying attention to my instructions. The second level, *aware,* is described as being aware of our surroundings while remaining engaged in other activities. As you read this book you are still maintaining a level of consciousness in respect to your surroundings. It's possible to listen to the radio, be engaged in conversation, or cook while being conscious of your surroundings. The third level, *alert,* is a heightened state of awareness. For example, when there's a potential threat and your focus is on that possible danger. The fourth level, *alarm,* is your mental state when an aggressor is actively threatening or attacking you or another.

In his book *On Combat,* psychologist Dave Grossman uses colors to explain in even greater detail what the NRA calls levels of awareness. He describes possible mental conditions as follows:

- White
- Yellow
- Red
- Black.[58]

Condition White

In **Condition White** you are unprepared to engage in a gunfight. Like the *unaware* condition you are oblivious to any threat or imminent attack. Condition White is okay when

---

[57] (The National Rifle Association, 2012, pp. I-6)
[58] (Grossman, On Combat, 2008, pp. 30-49)

in a safe place and not armed. Condition White is for home, play, and entertainment. Most Americans live in Condition White. The vast majority of people are oblivious to their surroundings. Not long ago I went out to eat with a friend. At the restaurant I noticed a man at a table twenty feet away who had a holstered pistol on his side in plain sight (Idaho is an open-carry state). It wasn't a small pistol; it was a full-sized Glock. Later, I asked my friend if he saw the man with the gun in the restaurant. He never noticed the man—Condition White.

In the spring of 1991, I was assigned to San Antonio's east side working a 5 pm to 3 am patrol shift. On April 18th, at about one am, I was dispatched to an apartment complex for a family disturbance. The dispatcher said the complainant's boyfriend was at the location and was threatening to shoot her. Officer Bob Bettis volunteered to back me up; minutes later Bettis and I arrived and located the apartment. Barbara, the complainant, said her boyfriend, Leander Floyd Jr., had just left on foot armed with two handguns. I radioed a description of Floyd over the police radio and warning that he was armed. Bettis and I searched, but were unable to locate him. Returning to the apartment, I told Barbara we couldn't find Floyd. Barbara decided to leave and stay with her mother. After seeing Barbara safely away, Bettis and I returned to service. At 3 am our shift ended.

Fourteen hours later, at 5 pm, on April 18th, 1991, Officer Bettis and I were at roll-call. We figured it to be a busy night; so right after roll call we decided to grab a cup of coffee and something to eat. We went to the Iron Skillet restaurant, sat down and ordered. Moments later the police emergency tone sounded over our radios followed by the most unsettling thing a police officer can hear, *"Shots fired! Officer down."*

Twenty-six year old uniformed Officer Doug Goeble was eating at a Church's Chicken restaurant. Doug recently asked for his girlfriend's hand in marriage and was looking at wedding ring advertisements while he ate. Outside in the parking lot Floyd and Barbara were arguing. Doug didn't notice the disturbance—Condition White. Floyd entered the restaurant, walked up behind Doug and shot him in the back of the head. Barbara ran into the restaurant hoping to find help. As Floyd was leaving he turned and shot Barbara several times in the back and fled on foot. I arrived to find both Doug and Barbara lying face down on the floor in pools of their own blood. Barbara was pronounced dead at the scene. Emergency Medical Technicians transported Doug to the hospital where he died two days later. Hours after the shooting, Floyd was apprehended. He received a life sentence for the two murders and remains in the custody of the Texas Department of Corrections.

Condition White is unacceptable for any on-duty police officer. Officer Goeble was a fine officer and was known to remain tactically aware. However, it was clear he was distracted by the excitement of his recent engagement. Grossman says Condition White is for the protected, not the protector. People in church are in Condition White. Church is safe. Church poses no threat. Church is where sheep gather—and that's okay. In fact, that's what pastors want. As a pastor, I want those gathered to hear the Word of God to feel safe. People can better learn in a safe environment. If Americans felt physically threatened at church how many would go? But more than *feeling* safe, I want them to *be* safe. Just like on-duty police officers, Condition White is unacceptable for members of an armed Safety Response Team. Members need to explain their need to remain vigilant to friends and family. This doesn't mean SRT members need to be callous or unfriendly, it means they need to remain aware of the surroundings and be aware of people or things that are out of place, seem odd, or may pose a threat; this is called Condition Yellow.

Condition Yellow

Condition Yellow is the next step up the ladder of mental preparedness. The main difference between Condition White and Condition Yellow is psychological, not physiological—it's being mentally in the game. Grossman describes, "When you move up to a level of basic alertness and readiness, a place where you are psychologically prepared for combat, you have entered the realm of 'Condition Yellow.'"[59] Most people will never notice a person in Condition Yellow. In fact, those likely to notice are only others trained to be aware and those who know a person best.

When my wife Sherry and I first started dating she thought I wasn't interested in her—furthest thing from the truth. She felt this way because when we were in public she noticed my attention was split. While I paid attention to her, she also noticed I was always looking around. Only later did she realize it was second nature for me to be aware of my surroundings and the people in them. I learned the importance of this early on in my police career. Soon after becoming a police officer I was attending classes at San Antonio College, a large community college near downtown San Antonio. One morning as I was walking across the campus I heard someone yelling, "Officer Rupp, Officer Rupp!" Looking up to a second floor landing of an outside staircase I saw a young man waving at me, "Don't you remember me? You arrested me!" To be quite honest, I hadn't remembered him. But had I been in Condition Yellow I would have recognized his preoccupation with me. This was an early lesson for me to always be aware of my surroundings when in public.

Condition Yellow means being mentally in the game. Being aware of your surroundings and continually assessing

---

[59] (Grossman, On Combat, 2008, p. 30)

potential threats. Colonel Jeff Cooper, one of the foremost authorities on defense weapons, understands the importance of being mentally in the game. Colonel Cooper, in his classic handbook, *The Principles of Personal Defense*, observes, "The great majority of victims of violent crime are taken by surprise. The one who anticipates the action wins."[60]

> *"The great majority of victims of violent crime are taken by surprise. The one who anticipates the action wins."*—Colonel Jeff Cooper

Condition Yellow means facing the direction that's most likely to pose a threat. If you are outside a church building, then position yourself so you can observe the parking lot. If you're inside the church, then stand facing the entrances. In a foyer you may need to choose a side wall to back-up against in order to see people coming and going from outside the building and from the sanctuary. While the service is in session select a position that provides the best view of the entrances. Keep a clear path between you and the most likely place from which a threat will come. The larger the church the more complicated this will be and the greater need for more members on the team. Team members should not sit together, they should be strategically located to provide the best coverage.

Condition Yellow means to look for things that are out of place, such as someone wearing an overcoat on a warm day, a young man coming to church by himself, a car backing into a stall rather than pulling straight in, or parking in a way that just doesn't seem right. Things that may seem innocent should grab your attention because they're unusual.

Condition Yellow doesn't come naturally. It's a learned behavior; you must learn to be aware of your surroundings and possible threats. This requires the study of

---

[60] (Cooper, 1972, p. 24)

people and their habits. In the police academy the most important safety measure that was driven into us was "Watch the hands." The hands are what hurt, the hands are what kill. A firearm left alone will not harm anyone. So, where do most

> *"Watch the hands." The hands are what hurt you the hands are what kill you.*

people keep their hands? People in Condition White, i.e. your church members, will usually keep their hands visible and engaged in their activity or conversation. Nearly 90% of people are right-handed, so almost everyone you watch will have their right hand visible and engaged. Once you are able to recognize "normal" it's easy to spot "abnormal." Abnormal should trigger a response. Most often the response is merely a heightened awareness.

Let's say you're an armed SRT team member standing outside, keeping an eye on people arriving at church when a young man that you don't recognize pulls into the parking lot and heads for the entrance. The young man looks up, sees you watching him, and then suddenly stops and hurries back to his car. Unlocking the back door, he reaches for something on the rear seat. You begin to close the distance, advancing toward the suspicious man when he turns, Bible in hand and hurries toward the door, so he won't be late for worship. You smile and give him a friendly welcome as he walks past you. This is Condition Yellow—being mentally in the game.

Condition Red

Condition Red is for engaging an enemy; it's the place to be when facing interpersonal human aggression. When an athlete moves from mental preparation to competitive playing he has transitioned to Condition Red. Grossman says that in Condition Red there are several physiological changes that take place. In Condition Red the heart rate jumps to 115-145 beats per minute (bpm) and fine motor skills deteriorate. The good news is complex motor skills, visual, and cognitive reaction time are at their peak. What does this mean? It means Condition Red is the "optimal survival and combat performance level."[61] Condition Red is where you *want* to be when engaged in a gunfight. Condition Red means a threat is imminent or an aggressor is shooting. If Condition Red is where we want to be in a gunfight, how do we get into and stay in Condition Red? Training and preparation. Condition Red is why reality based force-on-force scenario training is necessary. Training and preparation are why Stephen Curry can take critical fourth-quarter jump shots from beyond the 3-point line with a defender in his face and consistently make the shot. In Condition Red training and preparation take over and we operate on "automatic pilot." Automatic pilot and other phenomena associated with Condition Red is discussed in more detail in Chapter five.

What if we don't train and prepare? That's when Condition Black comes into play.

Condition Black

Condition Black is the place you don't want to be. In Condition Black the forebrain (the thinking part of the brain) shuts down. "As you enter into Condition Black, your cognitive processing deteriorates, which is a fancy way of saying that you stop thinking."[62]

> *"As you enter into Condition Black, your cognitive processing deteriorates, which is a fancy way of saying that you stop thinking."*—Dave Grossman

---

[61] (Grossman, On Combat, 2008, p. 30)
[62] (Grossman, On Combat, 2008, p. 44)

Hence, the response of one of the victims of the San Bernardino massacre, "I didn't know what to do or say. I was just numb."[63] Increased heart rate enhances physical performance—to a point; after that tipping point, increased heart rate becomes counterproductive. Grossman says, "that even under the most ideal circumstances, above 175 bpm a catastrophic set of events begins to happen."[64]

Grossman explains that the human brain is divided into three parts: the forebrain, midbrain, and hindbrain. Each part has a unique and distinctive function. The forebrain is where we do our thinking, unlike animals that have no forebrain. The forebrain is where we reason, consider, and decide. On the other hand, our midbrain doesn't think so much—it acts. The midbrain "performs extensive reflexive processes." The hindbrain is responsible for keeping our bodies alive and functioning by ensuring that things like the respiratory and cardiovascular systems are working.[65] When we enter Condition Black our midbrain and hindbrain literally take control and we are incapable of rational thought. We act and react based purely on survival instinct. This may sound reasonable, but when you are working not just for your own survival, but also for the survival of others you need every ounce of rational, logical thought.

In Condition Black your response may be to: (1) do nothing (fright response); (2) run (flight response); or (3) even engage the threat (fight response). But, whatever the response, it will be without thinking. It will be a reflexive response. While humans may have a predisposition to a survival mode, we can only respond out of what has been "stored" in our midbrain. Fear is a natural response. If someone walked into a place of worship brandishing a gun the natural response is fear. As an armed protector, the idea is to

---

[63] (Live interview of unidentified victim of the San Bernardino shooting, Fox News, December 3, 2015)
[64] (Grossman, On Combat, 2008, p. 43)
[65] (Grossman, On Combat, 2008, p. 43)

have a *controlled* response to fear. A controlled response comes through training and preparation.

It's important to know these conditions aren't rungs on a ladder, which naturally progress from one to the next. Think of them as mental positions. Condition White is a "sleeping position." While you may be wide awake, you are mentally unaware of any potential threats and you might as well be asleep. Condition White is fine while in a safe place and you consciously go into Condition White. Condition Yellow is a mental "sitting position." You are relaxed, in conversation, listening to the preacher, or eating dinner with a friend at a restaurant, but you remain aware of your surroundings. Condition Red is a "combat position." You are taking positive action to eliminate a threat. The fight has begun and you stay in the fight until the fight has ended and the threat no longer exists. After the fight you will return to Condition Yellow.

Condition Black is unacceptable. Condition Black is for the untrained and unprepared. Proper training and preparation will help avoid slipping into Condition Black. But what if you do slip into Condition Black, is there any hope? Yes, remember Condition Black is brought on by physiological changes that result in an increased heart rate. To get out of it the heart rate must be reduced. Grossman says this can be accomplished by intentional "tactical breathing." Basketball players lower their heart rate by taking slow deliberate breathes just before shooting free-throws. Grossman recommends a four-count deep, slow, and deliberate sequence to lower an elevated heart rate. He encourages people to try it while reading through his breathing steps:

- In through the nose two, three, four. Hold two, three, four. Out through the lips two, three, four. Hold two, three, four.

70

- In through the nose deep, deep, deep. Hold two, three, four. Out through the lips deep, deep, deep. Hold two, three, four.
- In through the nose two, three, four. Hold two, three, four. Out through the lips two, three, four. Hold two, three, four.[66]

It is important to understand this is not meditative "Zen" type breathing. Kenneth Murray explains,

> [Grossman's tactical breathing] is a focused, on-purpose breathing drill that must be practiced and used regularly to have access to it at the Unconscious Competent [UC] level of cognition if it is to be the least bit useful. It will not be "remembered" during a life threatening event, hence it will not be accessible if not conditioned to the UC level. Very few people or organizations "get" this...it is a foot note. Yet it is one of the most important tools during a critical incident.[67]

Let's now look at how to get into and remain in Condition Red when the situation demands it.

Fear-induced, force-on-force, real-life scenario training

Fear-induced, force-on-force, real-life scenario training is critical to train our bodies to enter into Condition Red, while avoiding Condition Black. As discussed above, Condition Red is the optimal fighting level. At this level there

---

[66] (Grossman, On Combat, 2008, p. 332)
[67] (Murray K. , 2016)

are physiological changes that take place, one is an elevated the heart rate. Basketball players get elevated heart rates when they run up and down the court. In order to perform under these physically demanding conditions players train and prepare by physically exerting themselves. However, as we have seen with Stephen Curry, there's also a mental element to the game. Curry prepares mentally for specific situations that he anticipates by visualizing the situation and practicing the shot. You too must prepare in like manner for a gun battle, where the stakes are much higher.

After research revealed heart rate is significantly elevated during a gunfight police trainers responded. In an attempt to simulate real-life conditions police firearms instructors began having students physically exert themselves by doing exercises to elevate their heart rates before engaging the target. I remember attending early police in-service training in which we repeated shooting the qualification course-of-fire, but with exercises before each stage. The instructor would give the command, "Run-in-place until you hear the whistle, at which time you will stop, draw your service pistol and shoot three rounds. Ready, begin." As you would expect, the scores dropped considerably.

At the time this was advanced cutting-edge firearms training. It demonstrated how much harder it was to accurately shoot when out of breath (trying to maintain a proper sight picture when sucking for air is difficult for the best of shooters). But further research demonstrated there is a difference between an elevated heart rate brought on by physical exertion and one caused by fear. Grossman points out that physical exertion causes the blood vessels to open up, pumping extra blood to the muscles and providing much needed oxygen. The increased flow of blood throughout the body normally causes a person's face to turn beet red or become flush with color. However, a "fear-induced" elevated heart rate will usually cause the face to turn white or to lose color.[68] Hence the expression, "He turned white as a sheet."

There's a reason for this phenomenon. It's called "vasoconstriction." Rather than opening up (as during physical exertion), the blood vessels constrict, limiting blood flow. Grossman explains,

> We are not sure why this happens, but the current, dominate theory is that the physical demands cause the body to scream for oxygen while the vasoconstriction shuts down the blood flow that provides oxygen, causing the heart to beat ever faster while achieving very little.[69]

So what's the effect of vasoconstriction? A loss of fine motor skills. The phenomenon of vasoconstriction is experienced in the cold. When your body starts to get cold it automatically responds by restricting blood flow to non-vital extremities. God designed the body to understand that fingers and toes can become cold and even frozen, yet the body can survive—fingers and toes aren't needed to live. That's why our hands and feet get cold so easily. The result is a loss of dexterity. Fine motor skills are out the window. If you've ever tried to write down something while your hands are cold then you've experienced this loss of dexterity. Depending on how cold your hands are will make the task range from difficult to impossible. What's the take away? Fear-induced stress causes the loss of fine motor skills and decreases your ability to think through situations.

It was a busy, hot summer night on San Antonio's east side. I checked back into service after finishing a call, "41-01, I'm 10-8 [in service]." The dispatcher responded,

---

68 (Grossman, On Combat, 2008, p. 44)
69 (Grossman, On Combat, 2008, p. 44)

"41-01 make ### Runnels Street, in the Sutton Homes for a disturbance, man holding his girlfriend at knifepoint. Use caution, no cover available." Because of the high volume of calls during the summer months it was common not have not to have a cover or back-up officer available. I acknowledged and responded, "10-4, 41-01, I'm on the way." I arrived and found EMS technicians outside the first floor apartment. One of the technicians was peeking into the apartment through a window, "I think she may have the knife," he said.

Hoping the situation was defused and with my right hand on my holstered service revolver, I rapped loudly on the outer screen door with my left hand. "Police, open the door!" I commanded. The interior steel door slowly swung inward and standing not three feet away, with only a screen door between us, was a rather large woman standing behind a much shorter man. The woman's arms were tightly wrapped around the short man's body. They struggled for control of a seven-inch butcher knife and yelled at each other in Spanish. Drawing my revolver I pointed it at the man's head and demanded "Drop the knife!" I repeated over and over while pushing on the screen door, with my left hand in a fruitless attempt to open it. "Drop the knife, or I'll shoot!" The man refused. Unable to open the screen door I started to squeeze the trigger. I could see the hammer of the .357 magnum coming back...the knife dropped. Relaxing my finger I allowed the hammer to come to rest without discharging the gun. I holstered the revolver—"Whew, that was a close one," I thought. It was then I noticed the screen door opened out by pulling it; all the while I was trying to push on it. The man was arrested without further incident.

Why didn't I notice the screen door opened out in the heat of battle? Because my mind was focused on the immediate threat, the knife. Fear-induced stress decreases one's ability to think through all aspects of a situation. With all my focus on the knife and the protection of the victim my mind wouldn't allow my eyes to leave the threat and look at the screen door to determine why it wouldn't open.

How should we prepare if we know that in a fear-induced event (e.g. someone walks into the church with a rifle) both fine motor skills and reasoning skills will be affected? By using fear-induced, force-on-force, real-life scenario training.

Obviously real guns, knives, and ammunition can't be used in scenario based training, but something that comes close needs to be used. The question is, how can an instructor mimic the physiological and psychological changes that are induced by fear in a training environment? Grossman advises, "[W]arriors can (and must) be inoculated against this [fear-induced] stressor by experiencing force-on-force scenarios in which they shoot and are shot at by paint-filled, gunpowder propelled, plastic bullets."[70]

There are a number of tools police use for force-on-force training. These include paintball guns, airsoft guns, non-lethal paint marking ammunition, and laser guns. The Reality Based Training industry is constantly improving training and coming up with training devices to better mimic real-life situations. The best and latest technology is very expensive, but for relatively low cost a high level of training can be conducted. It's critical for team members to accept scenario training as serious training; this isn't paintball gaming or laser tag. The purpose for using projectiles is to increase arousal by the threat of pain. Pain-induced fear best mimics the fear brought on by interpersonal human aggression.

Kenneth Murray has written an exceptional book on putting together real-life scenario based training entitled *Training at the Speed of Life, Vol. 1*. I would be foolish to attempt to duplicate his work. Although his primary audience is law enforcement, the basic safety instructions and

---

[70] (Grossman, On Combat, 2008, p. 38)

concepts are applicable to SRT training. Also, it's essential to have a professional trainer conduct the training. Check with your local police department or sheriff's office for available trainers. Law enforcement may be willing to provide some guidance and/or have the names and contact information of trainers in your area. Another option is to send a team member to a course to learn how to conduct training and become a training instructor.

Active-shooter training for a church armed SRT will be different from law enforcement training. Police training is reactionary training, responding to active-shooter events that are in progress, two-thirds of which are over prior to the arrival of law enforcement officers.[71] Officers train on where to approach when responding to a facility, how to deploy (e.g. one-person response or wait for other officers), where and how to enter, what equipment to take, and myriad of other things. For the most part, if an aggressor shows up at church wielding a firearm, knife, or other weapon, the SRT will be right smackdab in the middle of it—immediately. They'll go from Condition Yellow to Condition Red and will need to respond immediately to prevent or stop the killing.

Scenarios should be simple and realistic, for example: church is in session, the bad guy comes in, the team responds. There are two basic types of scenarios: shoot and don't shoot. While there should be a variety of scenarios (man with a gun, man with a knife, man with other weapon, man with no weapon, etc.) the goal is to train the team to respond properly to each scenario. Dual training sessions with both the armed and unarmed SRTs are also necessary to ensure that each team knows the responsibilities of the other team.

---

[71] (Texas State University and Federal Bureau of Investigation, 2014, p. 9)

The implications of being involved in a shooting
Chapter 5

Farmer's Daughter Shooting

It was busier than usual on the evening of Thursday, March 17, 1988. I finished booking my prisoner into the downtown San Antonio jail and just after 9 pm I advised my dispatcher that I was back in service. I keyed the mic, "41-01, I'll be 10-8." On the way back to my patrol district I stopped by a Denny's restaurant hoping to grab a cup of coffee and finish up some reports. Before I reached the restaurant door, a call for a man with a gun came out in my district; the dispatcher called my number, "Forty one-O-one, respond to the Farmer's Daughter for a man with a gun."

"Ten-four, 41-01, on the way," Officers Mike Lacy and Christine Kraeger volunteered to back me up. The Farmer's Daughter was an old-time Country and Western dance hall that catered to an older crowd. For the five years I worked the district I never had any trouble; in fact I can't recall ever being dispatched there for a disturbance. The dispatcher provided more information while I was enroute. She said a black male in a blue and white van was in the parking lot. He possibly had a gun.

Lacy, Kraeger, and I arrived at the same time. I went inside to contact the club's plain-clothes security guard who reported the incident. The security guard said a black male driving a blue and white van had pulled up to the front of the club almost driving into it. The guard saw what he believed was the butt of a handgun on the console between the van's front seats. He told the suspect to leave, but instead the man drove to the parking lot and parked. The guard pointed out where he believed the van was located. I radioed the other officers and we approached on foot.

The van was parked facing away from us. We walked closer and I could see someone sitting in the driver's seat— a black male. He looked over his right shoulder and saw me walking in his direction; he quickly ducked, lying down across the console, where the gun was said to be located. I alerted Lacy and Kraeger. Lacy had swung wide and was approaching the right-front while Kraeger and I continued to approach the right-rear of the van.

The suspect was still out of sight when I stopped behind the van. Moving to the left (driver's) side with my right hand on my service revolver and my flashlight in my left hand, I shined light into the cab, ordering the suspect to show me his hands. The suspect suddenly popped up. "Place both hands on the steering wheel," I ordered. He placed his left hand on the steering wheel and kept his right hand out of sight. I ordered him twice more to show me his hands as I continued walking slowly up to the driver's side. Keeping his attention on me, the suspect didn't see Lacy on the other side of the van; but Lacy was able to see inside the van. Lacy mouthed "He has a gun." I drew my revolver and took a step back.

The two parking spaces on the van's driver's side were empty. Directly behind and parked perpendicular to the van a Chevy El Camino was parked (see figure 5-1). I backed away and took a position on the opposite side of the El Camino. Kraeger was to my right. Lacy remained on the other side of the van. The suspect opened the driver's door and exited the van. Stepping away from the van he stood facing me. Both his hands were at his side and in his right hand was a small single-action pistol. I knew the hammer needed to be cocked before the pistol could be shot. Pointing my .357 magnum service revolver at him, I order him to drop the gun. He refused. With his right thumb he was attempting to cock the pistol.

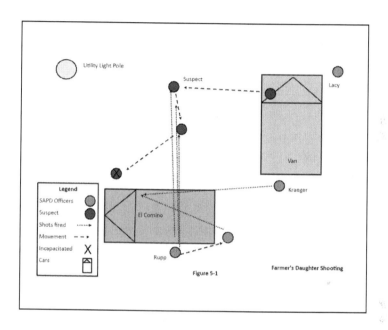

Figure 5-1

Thoughts raced through my mind. Things seemed to slow down. I was watching his hand with the gun in it, giving orders to drop it, and thinking about my wife Sherry all at the same time. We had been married less than two years. "Drop the gun!" I ordered. Ignoring my orders, he just looked at me with a blank stare. I pictured Chief Gibson driving up to my house to notify Sherry I'd been killed in the line-of-duty. He continued to stare. "Drop it, or I'll kill you!" I hoped the threat of death would get through to him. I could picture a hearse. Sherry dressed in black. People comforting her. He continued to stare. No! No, he wasn't going to do

79

this to Sherry. His hand started to come up. I pulled the trigger, he staggered toward me, and again I fired. He continued to come. He was almost at the passenger side of the El Camino; his hands were still moving. Now he was moving to my left. *Bang!* Another shot. The man dropped on the opposite side of the El Camino. I moved around and found him lying on the ground.

Laying on his left side he was looking at his blood covered right hand and his index finger that was dangling by a piece of skin. I moved in, still pointing my revolver at him. "I can see his hands, find the gun," I said. Lacy located the gun. Kreager and Lacy were okay and none of us were shot. The threat was over. We sought to administer first aid while notifying the dispatcher that we had been involved in a shooting and needed paramedics. Emergency Medical Services (EMS) transported the suspect to the hospital. Several hours later he was pronounced dead.

It was over. Or was it? What happens after the smoke clears? What are the after effects of being involved in a shooting? I had just killed a man, what now?

Immediately after the shooting I had trouble putting the whole event together. I didn't know how many times I shot; I thought I shot once or twice—maybe. Checking my cylinder, to my surprise, I found four spent cartridges. Four shots, did I even hit him? Was it Kreager or Lacy who shot him? We had department issued Smith and Wesson, model 65, .357 magnum revolvers and I didn't recall hearing any shots. There was no ringing in my ears. Where did my flashlight go? I remember having it when I walked up to the van, but I don't remember what I did with it. Looking around, I found it had rolled under the van. I must have dropped it when I drew my revolver, but I didn't remember doing so.

The follow-up investigation showed a clear picture. My first shot hit the suspect's right hand, the hand that held the pistol. Later, I found it's not uncommon for police officers to shoot a gun because that is where they are focusing.

My second shot hit him in the middle of his chest, the third shot passed through the passenger side bed of the El Camino and into his right leg. The fourth shot hit the rear glass of the El Camino. With the fourth shot I was tracking him as he moved to my left. Christine shot once, not hitting the suspect, Lacy didn't have a clear shot and didn't shoot from the other side of the van. I'd shot plenty of times on the range, but this wasn't a paper target. I'd hunted and killed birds, squirrels, and deer, but this wasn't an animal. This was different—this was a human being.

The taking of a human life is a serious matter. It seems to go against everything we've been taught from our Judeo-Christian values. Human life is different from all other forms of life. Taking the life of another human being is different from killing an animal. Only humanity was made in the image of God, *"So God created man in his own image, in the image of God he created him; male and female he created them,"* (Gen. 1:27).

In righteous judgment God destroyed human life in the great Flood. In his grace and mercy God saved Noah and his family through the great Flood. Following the Flood, God told Noah just how precious human life was. The value of something is determined by what it cost, Noah was told that a person who takes the life of another would have to pay with his own life. In Genesis chapter nine the Lord instituted human government and capital punishment, *"From his fellow man I will require a reckoning for the life of man. 'Whoever sheds the blood of man, by man shall his blood be shed, for God made man in his own image,'"* (Gen. 9:5-6).

Yes, the taking of human life is a serious matter. Nevertheless there is a time when the protection of the innocent involves killing an aggressor. King Solomon, the wise king and man of peace recognized this fact. Being inspired by the Holy Spirit he wrote,

81

"For everything there is a season, and a time for every matter under heaven: a time to be born, and a time to die; a time to plant, and a time to pluck up what is planted; a time to kill...." (Ecc. 3:1-3)

But not everyone is willing to pull the trigger.

The willingness to pull the trigger

Dying can't be undone. The human body can withstand severe abuse and torture, physically, emotionally, and mentally. But once a person is dead, there's no coming back.[72] Having been taught the value God places on human life, it's no wonder there's such a reluctance to kill in our society—even in the face of a deadly threat. Dave Grossman has done extensive study about the reluctance of soldiers on the battlefield to kill. After the rifle replaced the longbow as the standard issue weapon for soldiers the kill rate in war should have skyrocketed, but as Grossman discovered,

> The weak link between the killing potential and the killing capability of these units [military units armed with rifles] was the soldier. The simple fact is that when faced with a living, breathing, opponent instead of a target, a significant majority of the soldiers revert to a posturing mode in which they fire over their enemy's heads.[73]

Bill Jordan comments on the reality of facing another human being trying to kill you,

---

[72] This of course is in the natural order of things. God, who is above nature, can raise the dead back to life. Jesus is the prime example.

[73] (Grossman, On Killing, 1996, p. 11)

82

No normal man likes the thought of using a lethal weapon upon another human....You are struck with the realization that your opposition is a man who is trying to kill you and that in the next instant the world may have to find someone else to revolve about. His bullet may end life for you! Nothing in your prior experience, except gunfighting, can prepare you for this shocking thought.[74]

Kenneth Murray says this unwillingness to kill can be linked to police officers hesitating to pull the trigger in self-defense. Murray blames this on "societal preconditioning." [75] Although, if you watch what comes out of Hollywood you'd think Americans had no problem pulling the trigger. Murray notes, "Contrary to the relative ease with which TV lawmen dispatch the Tinseltown villains, killing another human being is not as simple as pointing a gun and pulling a trigger, although mechanically that's really all there is to it."[76] Humans, especially those raised in a Western Christian culture, are reluctant to take the life of another human being.

Mike Wood, in his tactical analysis of the Newhall shooting in which four California Highway Patrol troopers were gunned down, makes this observation,

The officers also had an additional challenge, because they were good men who were not immersed in a world of violence. They were raised in good families and were busy starting families of their own.... They fixed cars, attended barbeques, painted the baby's room, hugged their spouses, attended church,

---

[74] (Jordan, 1965, pp. 101, 105)
[75] (Murray K. R., 2004, p. 20)
[76] (Murray K. R., 2004, p. 19)

changed diapers, planned for the future, and did a million other everyday things completely unrelated to preparing for violent combat. They were raised in and lived in a culture that discouraged violence and stamped all kinds of hidden imprints on their brain that would cause hesitation to use force, even when it was justified and necessary.[77]

The simple fact is that without a willingness to kill the enemy our nation will not survive. Without the willingness of police officers to kill those wanting to kill us our society will not survive. From our American Revolution to our current war on terror and in the cities, towns, villages, and countrysides throughout our nation, America has always had those willing to face killers and kill them. According to Grossman, "The only thing that is holding our society together is the warrior.... Were we to go one generation without warriors our society would cease to exist."[78] Grossman defines a warrior as one who has the authority and capability to march toward the sound of the gun (face interpersonal human aggression) and return fire (operate under those conditions).[79]

> "Were we to go one generation without warriors our society would cease to exist."— Dave Grossman

The Bible has a lot to say about warriors and mighty men who fight and kill the enemy. First Chronicles 11:10-47 is a record of David's mighty men. The list includes: Jashobeam who *"wielded his spear against 300 whom he killed at one time."*; Eleazar who *"took his stand...and killed the Philistines."*; and Abishai (David's cousin) who *"wielded his spear against 300 men and killed them."* Why

---

[77] (Wood, 2013, p. 133)
[78] (Grossman, The Bullet Proof Mind audio seminar, 1995)
[79] (Grossman, The Bullet Proof Mind audio seminar, 1995)

does the Bible list these mighty men and give an account of how they killed so many in battle? Because they were warriors for Israel. They protected Israel against the enemy. These men weren't enshrined in the biblical record because they were killers, but because they were warriors who were willing to kill to protect God's people.

Where do warriors come from? Many people are unwilling to use deadly force against another human being, and that's okay. That's the way God has made them. We need these people. These are some of the finest humans on the planet. Perhaps King Solomon was one. The word of God shares an interesting story about David and his son.

> *David said to Solomon, "My son, I had it in my heart to build a house to the name of the LORD my God. But the word of the LORD came to me, saying, 'You have shed much blood and have waged great wars. You shall not build a house to my name, because you have shed so much blood before me on the earth. Behold, a son shall be born to you who shall be a man of rest. I will give him rest from all his surrounding enemies. For his name shall be Solomon, and I will give peace and quiet to Israel in his days. (1 Chr. 22:7-9)*

While I believe there's an innate sense in all humans to protect their own family, I also believe God instilled in the hearts of some a warrior spirit—the spirit of a protector. However, even in warriors there remains an averseness to use deadly force against another human being, which may cause hesitation. Whether this is a result of social conditioning or some other psychological factor, I don't know. The question is, "Can we tap into the warriors among us and give them the authority and capability to march toward the sound of gunfire and take action?"

Police Lt. James Como believes we can do this with a proper mindset and training by internalizing what he calls the "warrior spirit":

> If one is truly to become a warrior-protector, one must embrace the belief system and make it a life-style. It is inviting disaster if one believes that it is something that can be turned on and off at will. Only when one has truly internalized the warrior spirit can growth in the area of 'proactive' self-defense and tactical decision-making begin.[80]

Grossman continues this same argument when he explains,

> [M]odern training or conditioning techniques can partially overcome the inclination to posture. Indeed, the history of warfare can be seen as a history of increasingly more effective mechanisms for enabling and conditioning men to overcome their innate resistance to killing their fellow human beings.[81]

However, prior to training the mind and body, the soul needs to be at peace. Before being accepted as a member of an armed Safety Response Team, potential members must be asked, "Are you willing to kill another human being?" If the answer is "No", that's okay, but they cannot be on the team. They may be great for the unarmed or the medical Safety Response Team, but not the armed team.

---

[80] (Como as quoted by Murray, 2006, p. 20)
[81] (Grossman, On Killing, 1996, p. 13)

Let me reiterate here. The goal of the armed SRT is to quickly neutralize (that is to stop) an armed aggressor before the aggressor is able to harm any innocent person. To *quickly neutralize* is key. Response to an armed aggressor must be immediate and effective. To neutralize a threat is to nullify it. While the goal is to end the threat, it may cost the aggressor his life. Those willing to carry a gun to defend life must be willing to take it.

Not long ago the King James Version (KJV) of the Bible was the most widely used Bible in North America. The KJV's translation of the sixth commandment has caused undo stress for soldiers, police officers, and those defending themselves or others by using deadly force. The KJV translation reads, *"Thou shalt not kill"* (Exod. 20:13). *"Thou shalt not kill"* was often misunderstood as a divine and absolute prohibition against *any* taking of human life. However, as has already been demonstrated from Scripture, there is no absolute prohibition against the taking human life.

Later English translations of the Bible are more accurate when they use the word *murder* rather than *kill*, i.e. *"You shall not murder."* Kill is to take the life of another; murder is to do so with malice, that is, with evil intent. The Bible tells us God looks at our intentions or heart, *"For the Lord sees not as man sees: man looks on the outward appearance, but the Lord looks on the heart"* (1 Sam. 16:7). Jesus affirms the same in the New Testament saying that murder is a matter of the heart.[82]

Murder is to kill another human being without justification. The Hebrew word (רָצַח) translated as *kill* or *murder* can mean either. Therefore in Hebrew, like in English, context dictates which definition is intended by the writer. Numbers 35:30 is an example of this same Hebrew word (רָצַח) translated *kill* in the sixth commandment having different meanings in the same verse. Here's the KJV's translation

---

[82] (Mark 7:20-23)

where the Hebrew word (רָצַח) is translated as *murderer* and *death* in the same verse: *"...the murderer shall be put to death...."* The New Living Translation renders it: *"All murderers must be put to death."* In this text Moses uses the same word but means different things, he is saying a murderer (one who kills another without justification) is to be put to death (killed by the government with justification).

As noted before, all killing certainly cannot be against God's law or he would never have sanctioned and even commanded the deaths of Israel's enemies throughout the Old Testament. And even in the New Testament Jesus himself never condemns the Roman soldiers for carrying out all their duties. The command not to kill refers to unjustified killing that is outside the law[83]—we call it murder. The command not to murder is an absolute prohibition against the *unauthorized* or *unjustified* taking of human life.

Potential armed Safety Response Team members must understand that nowhere does the Bible prohibit the *lawful* use of deadly force to defend innocent life. It's the *unlawful* use of force that is prohibited in Scripture. However, even after knowing and acknowledging that there is no prohibition to use deadly force, a potential armed SRT team member must be willing to pull the trigger. After, and only after, the spiritual issue is addressed and put to rest can training begin.

In the Heat of Battle: Condition Red

In chapter four I presented the four levels of awareness. Grossman uses the colors white, yellow, red, and black to describe these levels of awareness. Condition Red is the "optimal survival and combat performance level."[84] Condi-

---

[83] (Stuart, 2006, p. 462)
[84] (Grossman, On Combat, 2008, p. 30)

tion Red is where you *want* to be when engaged in a gun-fight. However, getting into and staying in Condition Red takes training and preparation to overcome obstacles that prevent or hinder one's optimal awareness level. One obstacle affects almost every single person.

There is an innate fear in nearly every human being. It's the fear of interpersonal human aggression. Grossman calls the fear of interpersonal human aggression the "Universal Human Phobia."[85] A phobia is more than rational fear. The Farlex Partner Medical Dictionary defines phobia as "any objectively unfounded morbid dread or fear that arouses a state of panic."[86] A person in a state of panic isn't thinking straight, or isn't thinking at all. Responding to fear is one thing, having a phobic-scale response is another. Grossman uses the following example. If a person walked into a crowded room with a pistol and started shooting someone in the room, "up to 98 percent of the average audience [the others in the room] would experience a true phobic-scale response."[87] In other words, 98 percent of the people in the room would have a response that is irrational. Someone must have a *rational* response to stop the person from shooting others. It's not time to talk, to negotiate, or even to pray—it's time to act and to react effectively. To stop the killing someone must respond rationally. Police Lt. Como comments,

> Many a martial artist and marksman has found out, to their dismay, that merely prac-ticing a technique or drill over and over again, while ignoring the psychological as-pects of combat, most often had the opposite

---

[85] (Grossman, On Combat, 2008, pp. 2-7)
[86] (Farlex Partner Medical Dictionary, 2012)
[87] (Grossman, On Combat, 2008, p. 3)

result of what the intense training was meant to instill.[88]

A trained, prepared, and properly equipped protector in the above example would have been in Condition Yellow and at the sight of the pistol immediately moved to Condition Red. Then he or she would have taken action—quick action—to stop the aggressor. The protector needs to have a plan in place *before* an incident occurs so the response is both reflective and automatic.

> *The protector needs to have a plan in place* before *an incident occurs so the response is both reflective and automatic.*

By now, I hope I've established the necessity to take immediate and appropriate action to stop an aggressor. In order to do so, one must be *able* to take action. As discussed in chapter four, there are physiological changes the body experiences in the heat of battle for which we must be prepared (i.e. increased heart rate, vasoconstriction, and loss of fine motor skills). Like athletes that prepare to perform at the highest level when the game is on the line, members of an armed Safety Response Team also need to prepare to perform. Training and preparation are necessary to get in a fighting mindset (Condition Red) and stay there for the duration of a gunfight.

One critical form of preparation is Reality Based Training. The idea is to transition from Condition Yellow to Condition Red, the optimal "fighting zone" smoothly and quickly. In Condition Red your heart rate increases, enabling you to react more effectively with a heighted sense of awareness. However, there's a tipping point. At some point the heart rate increases too much, usually in excess of 175 beats

---

[88] (Como as quoted by Murray, 2006, p. 20)

per minute.[89] A sensory overload causes excessive heart rate and the effects of the increased heart rate turns negative and you slip into Condition Black. The idea is to respond from Condition Red when your body is at its peak—when you are in "a fighting mindset."

Perceptual Distortions

In addition to physiological changes there are also perceptual distortions that take place during a deadly encounter. Perceptual distortions affect the way things are *perceived*. A distortion means things are perceived other than as they are in reality. Perceptual distortions include hearing, vision, automatic responses, timing, freezing, and distracting thoughts. In some cases these perceptual distortions can cause the "fright" or the "numb-and-dumb" response of doing nothing, and/or other negative responses. But in other cases the distortions can produce positive sensory responses.

Dr. Alexis Artwohl has done extensive research on officer-involved shootings and how highly emotional experiences (i.e. being involved in a gunfight) impact perception and memory.[90] Many officers reported experiencing several perception or memory changes during a single event. See table 1 for her findings.

Training for a gunfight with Reality Based Training must be supplemented with knowing to expect sensory distortion during a deadly encounter. There are both positive perceptions and negative perceptions you may experience when engaged in deadly combat. While not everyone will experience every distortion, most will experience one or more. I experienced perceptual distortion in the Farmer's Daughter shooting detailed above. At the time of the shooting I wasn't familiar with Grossman's research. However,

---

[89] (Grossman, On Combat, 2008, p. 43)
[90] (Artwohl, 2002, pp. 18-24)

after hearing his *Bullet Proof Mind* seminar, I was an imme-diate fan. Eight years after the shooting I got answers to questions and was able to better understand the dynamics of a gunfight. Grossman has done extensive study on percep-tual distortions. Colonel Jeff Cooper explains in simple terms,

---

Perceptual Distortions

From *Perceptual and Memory Distortion During Officer-Involved Shootings*
By Dr. Alexis Artwohl
FBI Law Enforcement Bulletin
October 2002

- 84% heard sounds diminished
- 16% heard sounds intensified
- 79% experienced tunnel vision
- 71% experienced greater visual clarity
- 62% experienced slow motion time
- 17% experienced fast motion time
- 74% responded on "automatic pilot"
- 52% reported memory loss for part of the event
- 46% reported memory loss for part of their own behavior
- 21% reported memory distortion
- 39% experienced dissociation (i.e. a sense of detachment)
- 26% experienced intrusive distracting thoughts
- 7% reported temporary paralysis

Table 1

[M]any men who are not cowards are simply
unprepared for the fact of human savagery.
They have not thought about it...and they just
don't know what to do. When they look right
into the face of depravity or violence, they are

astonished and confounded. This can be corrected.[91]

Grossman admits there's a lot more research that needs to be done, but the current understanding is that changes to sensory organs are side effects of vasoconstriction.[92] For a more detailed discussion see his book *On Combat*. Below I will share how just a few of Dr. Artwohl's noted perceptual distortions affected me, personally.

Hearing and Seeing Distortions

A four-inch .357 magnum revolver makes a lot of noise. Why then did I not hear five full-powered magnum rounds go off during the Farmer's Daughter shooting? Because I experienced *auditory exclusion*. Auditory exclusion is more than simply not hearing something because your attention is elsewhere. We've all experienced times when we didn't hear our name being called because we were captivated by a movie we were watching, a book we were reading, or when we were in an intense conversation with someone else. Auditory exclusion is not simply being distracted.

Dr. Artwohl calls this phenomenon *diminished sound* and describes it as, "...the inability to hear very loud sounds that a person ordinarily obviously would hear, such as gunshots. It ranges from not hearing these sounds at all to hearing them in an odd muffled, distant manner."[93] Auditory exclusion is a *distortion*. In reality, there was a loud noise, but you didn't hear it, or it was significantly diminished. Grossman explains,

---

[91] (Cooper, 1972, p. 17)
[92] (Grossman, On Combat, 2008, p. 54)
[93] (Artwohl, 2002, p. 20)

Not seeing or hearing something because you are concentrating on something else is a psychological manifestation. Whereas "tunnel vision" and "auditory exclusion" appear to involve both psychological "concentration" influences and powerful physiological effects caused by biomechanical changes to the eye and ear.[94]

Dr. Lewinski defines biomechanics as "the mechanics of biological and muscular activity."[95] Biomechanics are effected by either external or internal forces physically acting upon the body. In the instance of auditory exclusion there are internal factors that somehow either completely shut down or greatly muffle the report of the gunshot. Grossman terms this Type-1 Auditory Exclusion:

The auditory system appears to "blink" creating a biomechanical shutdown that protects the ears from ringing afterwards. However...Type-I Auditory Exclusion...does not happen when you are under the stress of competitive shooting. It only happens in the actual killing circumstances of recreational hunting and combat.[96]

This explains why I didn't hear the shots and felt no effects (i.e. ringing in my ears) of them afterwards. Why is it important to know this? It's important to understand that auditory exclusion is a common phenomenon in a gunfight and shouldn't take you by surprise. Some police officers report not hearing their own gunshots or those of their partner's and

---

94 (Grossman, On Combat, 2008, p. 54)
95 (Lewinski, Biomechanics of Lethal Force Encounters--Officer Movements, 2002, p. 19)
96 (Grossman, On Combat, 2008, p. 61)

believing their guns were either malfunctioning or their partner wasn't shooting.[97]

There's another type of auditory exclusion, which Grossman dubs Type-II. "Type-II Auditory Exclusion can happen when you are completely relaxed (i.e. not in an excited state) and appears to be a result of the body receiving two simultaneous and overwhelming sensory stimuli." This may explain why some people who witness a shooting say the shots sounded like a "popping sound." The stimulus of seeing (visual sensory) someone being shot overwhelms, overloads, and blocks out or diminishes hearing (audio sensory).

On the other side of the coin, there are intensified sounds where the gunshots are extremely loud and other senses shut down. "The eyes turn off, the ears turn on and, as one law enforcement trainer put it, 'You hunker down and die, blind and afraid.'"[98] That's not an appropriate response.

As mentioned in an above quote, *tunnel vision* is also common. Tunnel vision is the mind focusing so intently on one object that nothing else is seen. Think about closing one eye and with the other looking through a paper-towel tube. All you can see is where you are pointing the tube, that's tunnel vision. In gunfights it's common for officers to focus so intently on the threat (i.e. the gun) nothing else is seen. This is not necessarily ideal since there may be more than one aggressor or one aggressor may have more than one weapon. What if your focus is on a knife in one hand and you don't see a gun in the other?

Understanding tunnel vision is important; proper training can help eliminate it. Police firearms instructors are teaching "scan-down-scan."[99] Scan-down-scan or "scanning" is an exercise in which officers break their focus on

---

[97] (Grossman, On Combat, 2008, p. 56)
[98] (Grossman, On Combat, 2008, p. 62)
[99] We started teaching "scan-down-scan" at the San Antonio Police training academy in the 1990s.

the target and scan to the left and right, then "check their six" by looking behind them immediately after shooting each stage of the course of fire. The hope is, that in an actual gunfight officers will avoid or break tunnel vision by scanning for other threats.

Further, keep in mind the bad guy may also be experiencing tunnel vision when he suddenly realizes he's facing opposition by an armed protector. Dr. Artwohl's research revealed 8 out of 10 police officers had experienced tunnel vision[100] so it's highly probable the aggressor is experiencing it as well. Police officers are taught to sidestep either right or left in a gunfight. This allows the officer to step "out of the sight" of a gunman who is experiencing tunnel vision (and even if the gunman isn't experiencing tunnel vision, he now has a moving target).

Dr. Artwohl's study also revealed that some officers experienced a heightened sense of hearing and/or vision that were considered positive effects. It seems during times of emergency survival senses that are needed somehow intensify providing, for example, better hearing or seeing as the situation dictates. One officer reported that while the sound of the gunshots diminished he was able to hear the footsteps of his assailant.[101] Know that you may experience a heightened sense of hearing or seeing; that's good; use it to your advantage.

Automatic Responses

Why did I shoot four times? Because of training. The police firearms instructors taught me to shoot until the threat was over. One firearms instructor drilled into our heads, "Shoot until he stops doing what it was that caused you to

---

[100] (Artwohl, 2002, p. 20)
[101] (Grossman, On Combat, 2008, p. 64)

start shooting." I shot until the threat was over. When I perceived no more threat, I stopped shooting. This is described as "automatic pilot." Automatic pilot is responding to stimuli with no conscious thought of what actions to take, you simply react. It's like when you're driving and a child runs into the street, your right foot immediately goes from the accelerator pedal to the brake pedal without conscious thought. How many times have you stopped your car by removing your foot from the accelerator pedal and pressing the brake pedal? Each time you do so you are training your foot and leg what to do in an emergency. When the emergency arises, you react. One's reaction in a gunfight is directly related to training.

After the Newhall shooting the California Highway Patrol (CHP) changed their firearms and tactics training. One of the changes they made was removing cans from the range that were used to collect spent shell casings. In an effort to save clean-up time and keep the pistol range looking neat and tidy, during the course-of-fire students would carefully empty their spent casings from their revolver into a can before reloading.[102] So what's the big deal? Muscle memory. Any athlete is familiar with muscle memory training. Quarterbacks and receivers practice the same routes over and over. Basketball players practice free-throws over and over. Golfers practice their swing over and over. What you do in training is what you'll do when it counts the most. In the heat of battle is when the forebrain shuts down and the midbrain takes over—you operate on auto-pilot.[103] If the wrong thing is in your midbrain things go downhill, fast. Rather than drawing from muscle memory that will bring a quick and positive end to the event, your actions (or inactions) may very well lead to a less than desirable end.

---

[102] (Wood, 2013, p. 103)
[103] (Grossman, On Combat, 2008, p. 75)

This is why training and practice is critical. It's been said, "Practice doesn't make perfect; perfect practice makes perfect." The point being practice right so you will respond right. What you do in training and practice is what you'll do in an actual situation.

Time Distortions

Time distortions can manifest themselves by either slow-motion or fast-motion time. In the Farmer's Daughter shooting I experienced slow-motion time. As the suspect exited the van and stepped facing me it seemed like forever, while in reality the whole incident was over very quickly. Not expecting this, I actually remember becoming fatigued (or at least feeling I was fatigued) as we faced off and I was ordering him to drop his gun.

Former football running back for the Los Angeles Raiders, Marcus Allen, described a moment of slow-motion time he experienced in his famous Super Bowl XVIII 74-yard touchdown run. Allen said during the run everything seemed to slow down and he had all the time he needed to dodge defenders. Then twenty yards from the end zone, when the "threat" was over, his perception returned to regular speed.[104]

Slow-motion time is a good thing, but you need to be aware it may occur. If it does, use it to your advantage. Our brains are capable of processing information at speeds we can't fathom

Fast-motion time isn't good. This is when things seem to be going so fast we don't have time to react. We are behind the curve and frantically trying to catch-up as we process what is happening. Fast-motion time is a result of being unprepared to respond in an appropriate way (lack of proper training) and/or being taken by surprise, such as being

---

[104] (ESPN Sports, 2012)

caught in Condition White. While your mind is processing, "There's a man with a gun, in church, and he's pointing it at people. That's not right." The aggressor is already shooting people even as your mind is telling you, "You have a gun. You have been trained. Respond." If, on the other hand, you are in Condition Yellow, being aware and half-expecting something might happen, then when you see the man with the gun your mind says, "Man with a gun. Respond." And you do, like stepping on the brake pedal.

Freezing or temporary paralysis

Freezing or *temporary paralysis* is cognitively coming to a stop and being unable to function. It's the "numb-and-dumb" response, and clearly ineffectual. When our response is no response, we have shut down completely.

> [S]ome officers perform poorly in combat because they are victims of uncontrollable physiological changes in their bodies. These changes can alter or shut down some cognitive processes entirely, can make them freeze in place when they should be moving, and can also dramatically impact basic senses like sight and sound, which can corrupt or block the information an officer needs to make proper and timely decisions and take precise actions.[105]

While freezing seems to be a death note, there is some good news. In Dr. Artwohl's study only seven percent of officers experienced freezing or *temporary paralysis.* That tells us that when someone is trained and prepared

---

[105] (Wood, 2013, p. 121)

there's a 93 percent chance they will not experience temporary paralysis. But there's more good news. Dr. Artwohl discovered that often the freezing is for a very short time. Dr. Artwohl, "...found that, in fact, this was simply the normal 'action-reaction' gap that occurs because the officers can shoot only after the suspect has engaged in behavior that represents a threat."[106]

Distracting Thoughts

In Dr. Artwohl's study, she reports that 26 percent of the officers involved in a gunfight had *intrusive distracting thoughts*. She defines intrusive distracting thoughts as, "those not immediately relevant to the tactical situation, often including thoughts about loved ones or personal matters."[107] On their face, intrusive thoughts appear to be negative. Dr. Artwohl even defines them with two adjectives: *intrusive distracting* thoughts. But, I suggest the two adjectives can be separated. In other words, *intrusive* thoughts are not necessarily *distracting* thoughts. How long does a thought take? What kind of thought is it? In my case the intrusive thoughts about my wife weren't distracting, in fact, I believe they spurred me on to make the right decision. During the Farmer's Daughter shooting, I experienced intrusive thoughts about San Antonio Police Chief Gibson going to my house and telling Sherry I'd been killed in the line-of-duty. Chief Gibson never made that trip to my house. Sherry and I now have three children and several grandchildren. None of whom may have ever been born if I hesitated.

Grossman's research supports my thoughts,

---

[106] (Artwohl, 2002, p. 21)
[107] (Artwohl, 2002, p. 21)

In the heat of battle, many warriors think of their family. One police officer said that during a gunfight, he had a vision of his three-year-old boy.... These intrusive thoughts are not always distracting, sometimes they can serve as an inspiration or motivation.... He [the officer] says that a sudden thought about his young son motivated him to get up [after being shot in the face] and return fire, killing his assailant.[108]

While the cause of these sensory distortions aren't fully understood we understand they happen during deadly combat incidents, when we are in a heightened state of emotional arousal. Dr. Artwohl's research noted that neither she nor others conducting similar studies measured other distortions such as distance, color, face recognition, or lighting distortions. When fighting for survival strange things happen to our bodies. These changes are both physiological and perceptual. Some are beneficial and some are detrimental to our survival and a successful outcome. Training and preparation will help overcome the negative effects and help us take advantage of the positive effects.

Picking up the Pieces

Not only do we need to be aware of the physiological and perceptual distortions during the heat of battle, we need to be aware of them when we are trying to pick up the pieces after the smoke clears. Likely you won't recall everything after the event for some time, if ever. Dr. Artwohl found that "...the body of research on perception and memory supports

---

[108] (Grossman, On Combat, 2008, p. 99)

the fact that people rarely are capable of total and perfect recall of events."[109]

It is important to understand that if you are involved in a gunfight you will likely have memory gaps. While there are certain things that are "burned into" your memory, there are other things you just won't recall. The follow-up investigation by law enforcement will help to fill in the gaps, but understand you may not be privy to this information for some time.

In his book *On Killing,* Grossman asked the question, "What does it feel like to kill?" He answers with five basic stages to killing: (1) the concern stage, (2) the actual kill, (3) exhilaration, (4) remorse, and (5) rationalization and acceptance.[110] In stage one, *the concern stage*, you wonder if you will be able to respond properly at the moment of truth. If you are honest with your willingness to pull the trigger coupled with proper training and preparation be confident that you will respond properly in the heat of battle. Stage two, *the actual kill*, is "simply" applying your training at the moment of truth and knowing that the goal isn't to kill, but to stop. Stage three, *exhilaration*, may not be experienced by everyone. Exhilaration is experienced because you won. You were just in a gunfight and you survived. I experienced this immediately after the Farmer's Daughter shooting. It helped that no innocent persons were hurt or killed. Nevertheless, I felt guilty about feeling good. At the time I didn't know this was a "normal" and acceptable response. Stage four, *remorse*, may also not be experienced by everyone. At the risk of not being thought of as a loving Christian, I never felt remorse. I was more pragmatic after the shooting—realizing he was attempting to shoot me; I shot him first.

---

[109] (Artwohl, 2002, p. 18)
[110] (Grossman, On Killing, 1996, pp. 231-240)

The fifth stage is critical, *rationalization and acceptance*. This is where you understand the necessity for doing what you did and accept it. If someone enters your church and threatens to kill he is responsible for what happens to him. Remember the lists of warriors in the Bible? These men are forever memorialized by the Lord in his holy Word for their willingness to stop bad people by killing them, thus stopping them from killing others.

Family members and friends will be interested in what happened. They'll want to know all the details. Now is the time to explain to your spouse, pastor, parents, or closest friend what to expect if you are involved in a shooting. Sharing is important, but you need to share with those who will not question or judge your actions. "Why didn't you shoot him in the leg?" "Why didn't you tell him to drop the gun?" Why questions are not what you need. Obviously, if you are a member of a Safety Response Team you have the support of your clergy and church leadership. That's whom you need to share with, and hopefully they will be familiar with what you are going through (share this book with them *before* something happens).

If you are a family member, friend, or clergy of a person involved in a deadly force encounter, please recognize their need for support. A safe person to talk with may also be needed. Let them tell you as much as they would like to share. Realize they may be feeling guilty, especially if others were harmed or killed. This "survivor's guilt" is normal. Encourage them and give them permission not to feel guilty. They responded as best they could and survived. There's no reason to feel guilty about winning a gun battle. Your affirmation is vital!

Use of Force policy/Federal and State law

Federal law is governed by the US Constitution, the Second Amendment says,

A well regulated Militia, being necessary to the security of a free State, the right of the people to keep and bear Arms, shall not be infringed.

Many Christians believe it is the government's responsibility to protect us. By passing the Second Amendment the government acknowledged its inability to adequately protect each individual and has given us the responsibility and authority to protect ourselves.

Lethal use of force laws in defense of life varies from state to state. However, most are generally the same: deadly force is justified to stop the imminent and unlawful use of deadly force, or force that would cause serious bodily harm against an innocent person. That innocent person can be the person using the deadly force (i.e. a member of the SRT) against the aggressor or another person (i.e. a church member).

According to the FBI website,

FBI special agents may use deadly force only when necessary—when the agent has a reasonable belief that the subject of such force poses an imminent danger of death or serious physical injury to the agent or another person. If feasible, a verbal warning to submit to the authority of the special agent is given prior to the use of deadly force.[111]

Notice the FBI use of force requires the agent to have "a reasonable belief" the danger is "imminent." Both reasonable belief and imminent danger must be present. Someone standing up in the middle of a service and yelling, "I hate

---

[111] (The Federal Bureau of Investigation, 2015)

God and all you people" isn't putting people in imminent peril. However, that same person standing up and yelling, "I hate God and all you people" while brandishing a gun would be perceived as putting people in imminent peril. One key in self-defense laws is that of reasonableness. The person using deadly force in self-defense or defense of another must be acting reasonably. This means the fear of great harm or imminent death that you experience must be sufficient enough to cause a *reasonable* person in the same or similar circumstances to feel that same fear; and that fear would cause a reasonable person to use deadly force. Further, you must act on the imminent fear alone, not on anger or revenge.

Consult your state penal code for the laws governing where you live. If you look for the information from the internet make sure you are on your state's website. Most will have a "dot-gov" ending such as "Idaho.gov". The state law of Idaho that deals with legal jeopardy reads as follows:

> 19-202A. Legal jeopardy in cases of self-defense and defense of other threatened parties.
>
> No person in this state shall be placed in legal jeopardy of any kind whatsoever for protecting himself or his family by reasonable means necessary, or when coming to the aid of another whom he reasonably believes to be in imminent danger of or the victim of aggravated assault, robbery, rape, murder or other heinous crime.

Once the "imminent danger" is over there's no further justification for the use of force. For example, if the aggressor throws his gun to the ground, holds his hands in a surrender position, and says, "I give up," then although you had justification to shoot moments before (and may have), the threat of death and/or serious bodily injury is over, as well as the justification for using deadly force.

Civil liabilities

What about the civil liabilities of having an armed Safety Response Team? As a senior pastor and former police officer, I understand and appreciate the concerns of civil liability. While we need to be aware of liabilities, it drives me crazy when the fear of a lawsuit drives policy. Our first and foremost consideration should be the safety of those who come on our property. If fire extinguishers and a sufficient number of exits weren't mandated would we still have them? I hope to think we would. Not to avoid liability, but to avoid injury or death. We shovel the snow off the sidewalks and put down ice-melt, not to avoid liability, but to provide a safe environment for our parishioners and guests.

That being said, when considering the possible liability of implementing an armed SRT, consider also the civil and real liabilities of not having one. A friend of mine was attending a church whose leadership was considering an armed security team. He told me that if they didn't implement one he was looking for another church. My friend often works on Sundays and is unable to attend church with his family on a regular basis. He felt that in today's environment it is incumbent on churches to provide physical protection for his family from an armed aggressor while they attended church.

Insurance companies see the necessity to have a plan in place in the event of an attack. Brotherhood Mutual, a leading insurer of churches writes this on their website:

> Brotherhood Mutual Insurance Company urges all churches to have a violence response plan—one that helps you respond swiftly and appropriately to threats against

people. Each church, however, must determine individually whether its set of circumstances merits an armed security team.[112]

Can an individual member be sued separately from the church? Yes. A person can be sued at just about any time for anything. We've all heard about the often ridiculous lawsuits that tie up the courts, yet we continue to be involved in activities that we may be sued for—driving, working, owning a home, etc. While we may take precautions, we don't radically change what we do day-to-day because we fear being sued. I'll protect my family from an intruder coming into my home and I won't worry about being sued. The way to avoid successful litigation is to be properly trained, prepared, equipped, and act as a reasonable person would act given the same set of circumstances.

---

[112] (Brotherhood Mutual, 2015)

Firearm Basics
Chapter 6

My first fast draw

In the early 1980s, retention duty-holsters (so named because of their design to prevent someone from snatching an officer's gun from the holster) were just becoming popular. One of the "lessons" prisoners were learning behind bars was to take police officers' guns away from them and use it on the officers. This put the manufacturers of police duty-holsters in a dilemma. They could manufacture a holster for a "quick draw" and could manufacture a holster for ultimate security. But could one holster do both? The goal of a retention duty-holster is to allow the handgun to be drawn safely and quickly by the officer while making it difficult for someone else to remove the gun from the holster. In order to achieve this goal, retention holsters have special buttons, snaps, straps, bands, and a slew of other specially engineered release devices.

In 1983 the San Antonio Police Department issued the duty revolver, but cadets were responsible to purchase their own holsters. I opted for one of the new retention holsters manufactured by Safariland®. During the police academy I trained and practiced drawing from the holster and continued to practice after graduation. But in the back of my mind was an ever-present nagging question, "Would I be able to draw my revolver quickly and smoothly at the moment of truth?"

One Sunday afternoon, shortly after graduation from the police academy, I was assigned to district 1-1 patrolling the downtown area. It was a slow and peaceful afternoon; the police radio was silent and there was little traffic as I drove past a white male walking alone. Walking the same direction I was driving, I could see he had his left hand in the front pocket of his gray hoody, and his right hand swinging naturally at his side. As I drove past he glanced at me with a nervous look. I noticed a curved metal band that looked like the back strap of a revolver in the hoody pocket. Making four right turns I came up behind him again and notified the dispatcher, "1-1, I'll be out at Lexington and St. Mary's with a white male, who possibly has a gun." "Ten-four, 1-1," the dispatcher responded.

After pulling up behind the suspect, I stopped and put my patrol cruiser in park. I opened the driver's door, took a position behind the door, and as I was yelling for the suspect to stop I noticed my revolver was already in my hand pointed at the threat. Without thinking I had drawn my revolver quickly and smoothly at the moment of truth. The suspect complied with my commands and I discovered that the metal band I thought might be a handgun was actually part of a Walkman® radio he had just stolen.

After that incident, I never again had that nagging concern about not being able to draw my service handgun quickly and smoothly when necessary. Training and preparation had paid off.

The early 80s also saw a large shift in police firearms training. By 1983 police were taking significant strides to move from marksmanship training to combat pistol training. Fourteen years earlier, in 1968 when California Highway (CHP) Patrol Trooper Gore was a cadet, the CHP academy focused on marksmanship. Marksmanship teaches the basics of how to safely and accurately shoot at a paper target. Cadet

Gore was good; in fact Gore finished at the top of his class.[113] The other three officers killed in the Newhall shooting were also accomplished marksmen. Then why were two ex-convicts able to out shoot and gun down four troopers? Because a gunfight is different from target shooting.

The two assailants had trained themselves to fight with guns. As has been demonstrated earlier, and as anyone who has been in an actual gunfight will attest to, shooting at a human being that's trying to kill you is far different from shooting at a paper target in a controlled environment. Mike Hall saw firearms training as a key reason for the Newhall massacre. At the time the CHP taught cadets marksmanship, but they didn't teach handgun combat skills, "The only trouble is that the CHP's program was oriented toward teaching marksmanship, while what Cadet Gore really needed was training in how to fight with firearms, a different matter entirely."[114]

This is offense, not defense. When the bad guy comes— Condition Red.

A gunfight is just that, a fight with guns. Longtime war correspondent John Steinbeck observed, "This is the law: The purpose of fighting is to win. There is no possible victory in defense. The sword is more important than the shield, and skill is more important than either. The final weapon is the brain. All else is supplemental."[115] Firearms expert Massad Ayoob agrees, his third priority of

> *"The purpose of fighting is to win. There is no possible victory in defense."*—John Steinbeck

---

[113] (Wood, 2013, p. 156)
[114] (Wood, 2013, p. 157)
[115] (Murray K. R., 2004, p. 14)

111

survival is "Skill with Safety Equipment".[116] One must be familiar with and able to use his or her equipment. This means each member of the team needs to be competent and proficient with his or her handgun. Marksmanship proficiency is necessary, but marksmanship is only the first step. You must learn how to fight with a gun. You must be able to demonstrate the skill necessary to not only shoot accurately, but to properly and effectively use your handgun in a gunfight.

Cardinal rules

Every training session, whether it's classroom instruction, Reality Based Training (using non-lethal guns), or actual live-fire training should begin with a review of the four cardinal rules of gun safety developed by Colonel Jeff Cooper:

1. Treat every gun as if it is loaded.
2. Never point the muzzle (the muzzle is the end of the barrel where the bullet comes out) at anything you are not willing to destroy.
3. Keep your finger off the trigger and out of the trigger guard until you are on target and ready to shoot.
4. Be aware of your target and beyond.

Rule number one, *"Treat every gun as if it is loaded,"* is violated on a regular basis. Far too often I've witnessed a person hand a gun to someone else and say, "Don't worry, it's not loaded." In my firearms training classes my son and I teach that it is the responsibility of both the person handing off the gun and the person receiving the gun

---

[116] (Wood, 2013, p. 124)

to ensure the gun is unloaded. It's not uncommon to hear media reports of someone being shot by a person who thought a gun was unloaded.

Treating every gun as if it is loaded means you should never violate rule number two, *"Never point the muzzle at anything you are not willing to destroy."* That seems so simple. Don't point a gun at other people, pets, TVs, couches, lamps, etc. Keep in mind, this rule also includes being careful not to inadvertently point a gun at yourself (including fingers, hands, or feet). If practicing dry-firing (dry-firing is detailed below) then ensure the gun is pointed in a safe direction at something that will stop a bullet.

Rule number three, *"Keep your finger off the trigger and out of the trigger guard until you are on target and ready to shoot,"* is the most common violation of the rules seen on the gun range. It's been my experience that the violation of this rule is the primary cause of unintentional discharges on the gun range. Shooters should learn to properly grip a handgun by running their trigger finger along the side of the gun (outside the trigger guard), pointed in the same direction as the muzzle. There's no need to insert a finger inside the trigger guard and on the trigger until on target and ready to shoot. Keeping the trigger finger off the trigger and outside the trigger guard will help prevent an unintentional discharge caused from a sympathetic response. A sympathetic response is an instinctive "knee jerk" reaction. Think about how fingers instinctively contract when a person suddenly reaches to catch an object. All four fingers and the thumb respond reflexively. The same thing happens when a person is startled—the fingers suddenly contract. What happens when a finger is on the trigger and the person is startled? *Bang!*

The fourth cardinal rule, *"Be aware of your target and beyond,"* is a common violation that occurs away from a controlled gun range. Most gun ranges have solid backstops designed to stop bullet travel and lessen the chance of ricochets. However, hunters and shooters (at a place other than a gun range), often violate this rule even when they think they're not. You must always consider where the bullet will travel to after it passes through the target, or if the target is missed. The bullet must be stopped—something or someone will stop it.

These four rules should be committed to memory and put into practice by everyone who handles any type of firearm.

Basic Marksmanship

Retired Border Patrol Assistant Chief Patrol Inspector, combat pistol instructor, and author Bill Jordan wrote:

> The only dependable way to learn to shoot a handgun is to start with deliberate, aimed, single action fire at a bull's-eye target until the fundamentals of trigger squeeze and sight alignment are thoroughly mastered. Only then should the shooter concern himself with fast double action shooting.[117]

Basic marksmanship skills should be demonstrated prior to combat pistol or tactical pistol training. Basic shooting fundamentals are:

1. *Stance.* Stance is the platform for shooting. A shaky platform results in a shaky shot. In marksmanship shooting there are traditionally two stances: the Weaver (standing bladed to the target, a right handed shooter shooting to the left) and

---

[117] (Jordan, 1965, p. 91)

the Isosceles (standing square to the target, the target directly in front of the shooter). For combat shooting the optimal stance is a modification of either of these by incorporating an athletic stance. Think of a boxer—feet shoulder width apart, knees bent, shoulders over the toes, and weight forward. One that lends itself to stability.

2. *Grip.* The grip should be a natural pointing grip. Thumbs along the side of the gun opposite the trigger finger, pointing down range. The grip should be firm, but not a white-knuckled-death grip. Don't attempt to completely stop the gun from moving. Anyone who has a heartbeat and is breathing will cause the gun to move.

3. *Sight alignment.* Sight alignment is the alignment of the front sight (sight at the

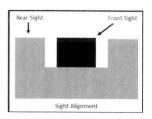

muzzle) and rear sight (sight above grips). The sights should be even across the top with even space on either side of the front sight.

4. *Sight picture.* The sight picture includes

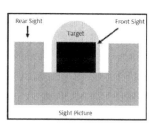

the sight alignment and the point of aim on the target. The human eye can

115

only focus at one distance at a time. It's impossible to focus on the rear sight, front sight, and the target at the same time. Focus on the front sight and use your peripheral vision to align the rear sight and target to the front sight; both the rear sight and the target will be out of focus. This may seem unnatural at first, since shooters are tempted to focus on the target. However, you must keep the focus on the front sight. Remember the gun will still move slightly, and the front sight may seem to "dance" a little.

5. *Trigger control.* To help control the trigger, trigger "slack" or "play" needs to be taken up. After the slack is taken out of the trigger the trigger should be pressed straight to the rear, evenly and smoothly. Shooters shouldn't attempt to anticipate when the hammer will fall and the gun discharges.

6. *Breathing.* Shooters should breathe normally, and then "cut-off" breathing when the trigger slack is taken up—just before the first shot is fired. You can shoot as many rounds as you are comfortable with before taking another breath.

7. *Follow through.* Follow through is maintaining a firm grip while allowing the gun to recoil and then coming back to position. Don't fight it, go with it.

Fundamental shooting skills can be learned in a rather short amount of time. Any competent firearms instructor should be able to safely and effectively teach almost anyone how to safely and accurately shoot a handgun. However, to maintain and increase fundamental shooting skills regular training and practice are necessary. One easy and inexpensive form of practice is *dry-firing*. Dry-firing is conducted with an **unloaded** gun in a safe place. Dry-firing is the exercise of practicing stance, grip, sight alignment, sight picture, trigger control, and breathing without shooting live ammunition. Follow through may even be simulated. Start by unloading the gun—double and triple check it to be absolutely sure. Once the gun is unloaded remove any live ammunition from the room in which the dry-fire practice will take place. After following these safety measures you are ready to begin training. The vast majority of modern handguns will not be damaged by dry-firing them. You can check with your gun manufacturer to confirm the safety of dry firing your particular handgun.

During dry-firing practice a "target" that will stop a real bullet should always be used. Even after all the safety measures, one cartridge may be missed (remember rule #2). In order to dry-fire a semi-automatic pistol the slide will need to be racked each time the trigger is pulled to reset the trigger. The purpose of dry-firing is muscle memory. Dry-firing should be done slowly and methodically. Every step should be thought through: stance, grip, sight alignment, sight picture, and breathing control. When everything is right, front sight is in focus—sharp and crisp, trigger slack is taken up, breathing "cut-off", then the trigger is slowly pressed rearward until the hammer falls (or sear is released). When the gun goes "click" the trigger should be held back. If using a revolver slowly release pressure on the trigger allowing it to go forward until it resets, repeat the dry-fire exercise. If using a semi-automatic, while continuing to hold the trigger back, rack the slide, get back on target and slowly release the trigger allowing it to go forward until it resets. Repeat the dry-fire exercise.

As you become more proficient going through the motions of proper marksmanship the speed of the exercise should increase a little at a time. Proper training and form produces good muscle memory habits. When the moment of truth comes the muscles will instinctively respond rightly. To those unfamiliar with marksmanship, dry-firing may seem silly, but I know of no accomplished shooter that doesn't practice dry-firing. In fact, there are now training guns available exclusively for dry-firing. These training aids allow shooters to practice safely and without needing to rack the slide to reset the trigger.

Live-fire training

When I was a police officer, the department required annual firearms qualification. Each year every officer attended a week of "In-Service" training at the police academy. One day, or at least half of a day, was dedicated to firearms qualification. (That most states require their police officers to qualify only annually comes as a surprise to many.) The normal procedure for "range day" was to begin with classroom instruction, reviewing shooting fundamentals. After being reminded about trigger control, sight alignment, sight picture, grip, stance, breathing, and so forth the officers headed out to the range. The range master would explain the course-of-fire and officers shot a practice course-of-fire to "warm-up". This gave the firearms instructors the opportunity to correct problems shooters were experiencing. Following the practice course-of-fire a qualifying round would be shot. The vast majority of officers qualified with an 85% or better. A 70% was required for qualification. The problem is real-life doesn't work that way. When an officer gets called to a disturbance no one stops them and says, "Hold on, at this call you'll be involved in a shooting. Let's go over the fundamentals of shooting and warm up with a few practice shots before you make the call." In the mid-1990s, when I was assigned as the sergeant in charge of firearms training we decided to change things. When officers showed up for

118

range day we had the class go immediately to the range, with no classroom instruction. When told the first course-of-fire was for qualification we heard the moans and complaints, "That's not fair, we need some warm-up shots." Needless to say the scores went down, but the firearms instructors had a better idea of the officers' skill—and so did the officers.

Members of an armed Safety Response Team must be proficient with the gun they carry. How should proficiency be measured? It's a given that everyone has room for improvement. And training and practice are necessary to maintain proficiency, but how should members of the team be qualified? There are a few options.

One option for qualification is to use the qualification course used by the state or local police or sheriff. Police annual qualification courses-of-fire are not that difficult, but they do require a level of proficiency. These courses-of-fire are generally about 50 rounds. Keep in mind that they may require reloading and may have to be adjusted for members of the team carrying guns with a limited number of rounds (i.e. a five-shot revolver). A second option is to require that all members have a concealed carry permit. However, I caution against this being the only qualification. In fact, I *warn* against this being the only qualification, especially when some states require no level of proficiency to obtain a concealed carry license. A third option, and perhaps the best option, is to use the FBI's pistol qualification course.

Former CIA officer and author of *The Covert Guide to Concealed Carry*, Jason Hanson, recommends the FBI course adopted in January 2013. Hanson writes,

> Every government agency likes to think they're the best. So whether or not you're a fan of the FBI, there is one thing the Bureau is good at... and that's keeping statistics on shootings. Over the years, the FBI has documented and studied thousands of shootings,

and in January of this year the FBI changed its qualification course based on the feedback of these shootings. In short, the old course involved shooting at far distances as much as 50 yards, but the new course focuses on close quarters shooting since the majority of gunfights occur at seven yards or less.[118]

See appendix "A" for the FBI's course of fire.

In his book, *Training at the Speed of Life, Vol. 1,* Kenneth Murray writes about a one-shot qualification advocated by former Orlando Police Department range master, O. Frank Repass:

Repass has extensive research and experience demonstrating that if you can hit a five inch by ten inch target that is hanging at a bladed angle, from a "ready gun" position at five yards in less than 1.5 seconds, you have mastered the use of your handgun to the level necessary for delivering swift and accurate fire under realistic conditions. After you have "qualified," the rest of the time spent at the range can be dedicated to learning how to fight with your pistol.[119]

Murray argues this moves firearms training from the traditional "*qualification* paradigm toward a competency-based demonstration of proficiency."[120] As of this writing, Repass' one-shot qualification hasn't been widely adopted by law enforcement. However, it should not be dismissed out of hand. Repass' one-shot qualification is a great marker of where someone is at in their proficiency with a handgun. The

---

[118] (Hanson, 2013)
[119] (Murray K. R., 2004, p. 25)
[120] (Murray K. R., 2004, p. 25)

distance (five yards), the target (5"x10"), and the time (1.5 seconds) all provide a realistic and achievable goal.

For years there has been a trend by law enforcement firearms trainers to move away from numeric scores to a "pass" or "fail" score. Firearms records of officers involved in shootings are routinely subpoenaed as evidence. Defense attorneys use scores to cast doubt in the minds of jurors as to officers' intentions and justification for using lethal force. If an officer is an outstanding marksman with high shooting scores, an unscrupulous attorney may question why more than half of the officer's shots missed in an attempt to show the officer was unsure of his or her decision to shoot. Although we know from research traditional marksmanship doesn't equal being in a real gunfight, jurors don't know that. On the other hand, if an officer scored the minimum (i.e. 70%) an attorney may attempt to question the officer's qualification to even be in law enforcement. By having a pass/fail scoring system all of a department's records are the same: passing. Those failing are disqualified from carrying a firearm until they pass.

While numeric scores have value in showing improvement in marksmanship, remember basic marksmanship is just the foundation for combat or tactical shooting.

Combat shooting

In earlier chapters I discussed the necessity of reality based training (RBT) to prepare mentally for a gunfight. In addition to fear induced scenario training with nonlethal training aids it is essential team members be trained in combat or tactical shooting. The goal of marksmanship shooting is to shoot as accurately as possible to achieve a high score. The goal of combat shooting "is to get a disabling hit upon

> *The goal of combat shooting "is to get a disabling hit upon your opponent before he can do the same to you, regardless of how you go about it."*—Bill Jordan

your opponent before he can do the same to you, regardless of how you go about it."[121]

Gunfights take place inside, outside, in open areas with no cover or concealment, to the closed quarters of a vehicle. Because every gunfight is different there is no one specific form or method of combat shooting. Bill Jordan in his book *No Second Place Winner* advocated point shooting or instinctive shooting and says the nature of combat shooting is governed by the situation. However, Jordan says the greatest single factor is *range* the second is *speed.*[122] The closer your opponent is the faster your reaction must be. As the range increases the more time you have to use the gun sights and obtain proper sight alignment.

Combat training needs to include shooting from very close quarters—from arm's length out to 15 yards. This is shooting without using the gun sights. The fact is, in a gunfight you will be focused on the threat, not your front sight. Survival instincts take over and just like with Reality Based Training combat shooting aims to give you something to draw from instinctively at the moment of truth.

Live-fire shooting positions

Live-fire training should involve shooting from these three positions: the low-ready, drawing from the holster, and the safety circle. Of paramount concern is muzzle awareness.

---

[121] (Jordan, 1965, p. 91)
[122] (Jordan, 1965, p. 91)

While handling any firearm always be attentive to where the muzzle of the gun is pointed!

Low-ready

A beginning shooter should first learn to shoot from the "low-ready" standing position. In the low-ready position the shooter is standing in their shooting stance, facing the target, holding the handgun with the proper grip, the hands lowered down to about a 45 degree angle from the body. At the command to fire the shooter simply raises their arms bringing the gun up to obtain a proper sight picture. After firing the shooter returns to the low-ready position.

Drawing from holster

After fundamental skills are learned, training to draw from a holster is the natural next step. Holster training should be practiced with an unloaded gun (or better, an inert training gun of the same model as the real gun) until a level of confidence and competence is reached. Start slow! As demonstrated in the above story of my first fast draw, speed will be the natural result of proper training.

Basic geometry teaches that the shortest distance between two points is a straight line. A straight line from the holster to the sight picture is the fastest and safest draw. Begin from the shooting stance with a proper grip on the holstered gun. See chapter seven for a better understanding of selecting a holster and ensuring a proper grip while your gun is seated in it. Slowly remove the gun from the holster while your finger remains outside of the trigger guard. At the same time bring your support hand over to your drawing hand to complete a correct two-handed grip as the gun is "punched" into a proper sight picture. Practice this several times until it comes naturally. You should be able to grip, draw, and get a sight picture without taking your eyes off the target.

Once a level of comfort is reached going from the grip to the draw, and then to the sight picture, it's time to move to the next level. Instead of beginning from a shooting stance move to making the draw from a more realistic one. For instance, start from a natural position like talking with someone in a normal conversation. Your hands should be relaxed at your side. From there you want to transition to the shooting stance, then draw, and obtain your sight picture. Again, start slowly and methodically. When drawing and getting on target from a natural posture becomes comfortable put on a jacket, vest, or shirt to conceal the gun, as it would normally be carried. With clothing covering the gun, you will need to learn to push or pull the clothing out of the way before obtaining a grip on the gun. Neglecting to practice with the gun concealed by clothing may cause you to grab a handful of clothing along with the gun at the moment of truth. Next practice drawing from a variety of other positions you may face (i.e. sitting, kneeling, or crouching).

Just a few minutes of daily practice will produce dramatic results. After becoming competent off the range, practice drawing from the holster during live-fire training.

Safety Circle

In addition to learning the low-ready position and drawing from the holster, the "safety circle" is a third critical position to learn. The safety circle allows for safely moving with a loaded gun out of the holster and ready for quick use. In the safety circle, the handgun is held close to the front of the body with the muzzle pointed straight down. To obtain the safety circle place the support hand just below the chest but above the stomach with the palm facing your body, elbow straight out, and thumb up. Using a proper grip on the gun in the primary shooting hand and muzzle pointed down, place the gun on top of the support hand with thumbs pressed against each other. From this position you are able to punch the gun straight out into a shooting position. This position is used for moving tactically either alone or with a team. It's called the safety circle because the gun is pointed down, in a safe direction, allowing someone to move in any direction without unintentionally pointing the muzzle at something they are unwilling to destroy (see Rule #2).

Safety Circle

In bygone times, the low-ready was the position of choice when moving, but the safety circle is safer for both individual and team movement. With practice the safety circle will become second nature.

Although these three basic positions should be mastered, you should also practice shooting from a variety of positions. The one constant in a gunfight is the inconsistency of your surroundings or circumstances. Advanced tactical training should include shooting from other positions such as kneeling, crouching, sitting, prone, back, etc.

Cover/Concealment

Cover and *concealment* are two terms that are sometimes confusing and erroneously used interchangeably. *Cover* is any object you are able to place between yourself and the aggressor that will stop bullets. The thick bullet-proof glass in a bank drive-through is cover, although its transparency doesn't provide concealment. *Concealment* is any object that conceals you from the aggressor's vision—

either completely or partially. Concealment may or may not be cover. Concealment can be a cardboard box, a wall, curtains, or a door. Concealment may even be darkness.

Interior house walls provide concealment, but not cover. Virtually all handgun calibers, including .22 caliber, will easily pass through two sheets of drywall. Furthermore, most will also travel through one or two 2x4 studs. Bullets will also easily pass through common interior doors and most exterior doors.

Part of situational awareness is recognizing what cover and/or concealment is available at any given time. Cover is better than concealment—concealment is better than nothing. It is good to recognize that even if concealment cannot stop bullets many people are either unaware that bullets will pass through most objects (such as pews, chairs, walls, etc.) and/or they will instinctively attempt to shoot around concealment. Therefore, use cover if available, but don't underestimate the use of concealment if cover isn't available. Also, the aggressor may be using concealment you can shoot through, but be sure of what is beyond the target. If the aggressor is behind a wall, who else is on the other side? If the aggressor is peeking over the top of a chair or pew to present a smaller target, recognize that a bullet can penetrate the chair or pew, offering a larger target to shoot.

Never hesitate to use cover or concealment, no matter how small or flimsy it is. At the San Antonio police academy cadets were put through a concealment scenario during police tactics training. Cadets were given the following scenario: "You have been pursuing a man wanted for murder and who has already shot your partner. He is armed with a gun and swears he won't be taken alive. During the foot pursuit you chase him into a room where you confront him. He's the only one in the room. There is no one else." With that information each cadet was sent into the room. As the cadet entered the room he found the bad guy hiding behind a long piece of cardboard held in one hand. With his other hand he was attempting to point his gun at the cadet from around the side of the cardboard. Many cadets attempted to maneuver around the cardboard to get a "clear" shot rather than simply shooting through the cardboard. The point of the exercise was to get the cadet to think about cover and concealment. Under the stress of the scenario many didn't think, "That's simply cardboard, I can shoot right through it."

The scenario aims to teach two important things: for the cadet (1) to know and be aware of the capabilities of the service ammunition; and (2) to understand the psychological advantage of using concealment. Just as the "bad guy" in the scenario used concealment to his advantage, so too should police officers. Cover is best—use when available; concealment is better than nothing.

Movement

"Action always beats reaction," the police academy instructor told our class. Unfortunately, the protector of innocent lives on American soil is, more often than not, reacting to an action and is therefore disadvantaged in a gunfight. Hence, the protector needs to gain any possible advantage—that advantage may be movement.

In the absence of cover or concealment, use movement. In the Newhall shooting the ex-convicts were constantly moving and shooting. All four officers that were gunned down took up static positions from which to shoot. The bad guys gained the advantage of shooting at stationary targets while the officers were shooting at moving targets. But in order to shoot on the move you must train using movement. As with any firearms training, begin with an unloaded or inert training gun.

Recall that in the Newhall shooting (detailed in chapter four) there was one other "good guy" who was involved in the shooting. Mr. Gary Kness, a former Marine, happened to be driving by at the time of the shooting. Initially, Mr.

Kness thought a movie was being filmed when he saw the two police cruisers and the red Pontiac in the parking lot. He decided to act after realizing he was witnessing a real police shooting, Mr. Kness bailed out of his car and ran to where Officer Allyen was lying wounded. Mr. Kness grabbed the officer's shotgun from the ground and tried to fire it, but found it empty. After attempting to drag the downed officer out of the line of fire he picked up Allyen's revolver and shot one time at Davis, hitting him in the arm. The next time Mr. Kness pulled the trigger it fell on a spent casing. Mr. Kness fled from the danger zone into a ditch when he heard the sirens of the responding patrols. He knew he might be mistaken for one of the criminals before he could safely make himself known to other officers.

In his analysis of the shooting, Mike Wood comments, "There are certainly many reasons why Mr. Kness avoided injury, but the fact that he was continuously moving while on the battlefield was certainly preeminent among them and constitutes a powerful lesson for today's warriors."[123] Moving and shooting is very dangerous and should only be attempted after receiving training and supervision from a qualified firearms instructor. However, because moving provides such an excellent advantage it behooves any possible armed SRT member to receive the necessary instruction and practice with it regularly.

Just as today's police move from marksmanship to tactical pistol training, so too should members of an armed Safety Response Team. Tactical or combat shooting is more than just standing and shooting at paper targets. It includes decision making, addressing multiple targets, moving and shooting, reloading, clearing malfunctions, and other types of shooting that better mimics a gunfight.

---

[123] (Wood, 2013, p. 153)

128

Equipment
Chapter 7

Miami FBI Shooting

In 1986 the Miami area was hit with a slew of bank robberies and a special Federal Bureau of Investigation (FBI) task force was assigned to the case. On April 11, 1986, eight FBI agents were involved in a gunfight that would, among other things, result in a change of FBI and law enforcement equipment.

The two bank robbers, William Matix and Michael Platt, were in a black Monte Carlo driven by Matix. The suspects were being followed by FBI agents Ben Grogan and Jerry Dove. Six other agents (in four other vehicles) were also following Matix and Platt. The decision was made to stop the suspects by forcing them off the road and blocking any escape route. The agents rammed into the Monte Carlo forcing it into the small parking lot of 12201 82nd Avenue in south Dade County. The suspects' vehicle was squeezed between a parked Oldsmobile Cutlass on their right and Agent Dick Manauzzi's car on their left. Grogan and Dove's car stopped about 20 feet behind the Monte Carlo. Supervisor Agent Gordon McNeill stopped his car perpendicular to and at the rear of Manauzzi's car (see figure 7-1).

As soon as the cars came to a stop gunfire erupted. Platt, armed with a Ruger mini-14, semi-automatic .223 caliber rifle starting shooting at Manauzzi. Unfortunately, during the car pursuit Manauzzi had placed his revolver on the seat between his legs for easier access. But, to stop the suspects he had to ram their vehicle twice, which caused his driver's door to pop open. During the impact Manauzzi's gun slid from the seat and he believed it tumbled into the street. When Platt opened up on him, the agent quickly ran

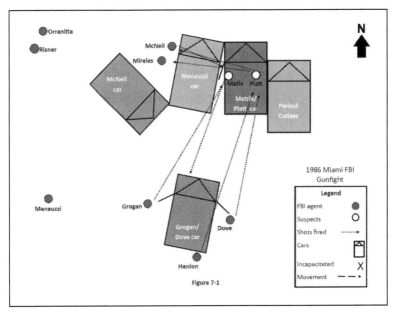

Figure 7-1

from his car and retreated to search for his lost revolver. Even though Platt fired several shots at Manauzzi's car, he was unable to get a clean shot at the agent. However, Manauzzi was hit with bullet fragments.

While Platt was shooting at Manauzzi, Matix opened his driver's door the few inches he was able, and fired a shot towards Grogan and Dove with a 12-gauge shotgun loaded with #6 birdshot. From 25 feet behind the Monte Carlo, they returned fire with their Smith and Wesson 9mm pistols.

Grogan hit Matix in the right forearm. The 9mm, 115 grain jacketed hollow point bullet traveled completely through Matix's right forearm, causing minimal injury.

Meanwhile, agents McNeill and Ed Mireles rushed to the front left fender of Manauzzi's car and immediately began taking fire from Platt. Mireles, armed with a Remington 870 12-gauge shotgun loaded with 00 buckshot, was hit in the left forearm from Platt's .223 and knocked down before he could get a shot off. Mireles was unable to use his left arm for the remainder of the gunfight. McNeill emptied his six shot revolver—a Smith and Wesson .357, loaded with .38+P hollow points—into the Monte Carlo and hit Matix at least twice. McNeill's fifth shot entered on the right side of Matix's head, just in front of his ear. The bullet came to rest in his maxillary sinus cavity. Dr. W. French Anderson believes this rendered Matix unconscious.[124] The injury caused Matix to slump down facing McNeill. McNeill's sixth shot entered the right side of Matix's neck, hit the bulk of neck muscles connected to the spinal cord, traveled downward and came to rest on top of (after hitting, but not puncturing) his right lung.[125] Matix was temporarily out of the fight.

Platt exited through the passenger window of the Monte Carlo while Dove continued to fire at him from the rear. Agents Gil Orrantia and Ron Risner, who were across the street and to the left and front of the Monte Carlo, were also shooting at Platt. In order to exit the Monte Carlo, Platt had to climb out the passenger window and on to the hood of the parked Cutlass. The exposed Platt was hit four times exiting the car. One shot from Dove's 9mm passed through his upper right arm, into his chest cavity, and into his right lung. A second bullet from Dove passed through his left foot from left to right. A third bullet was a through-and-through

---

[124] (Anderson, 2006, p. 25)
[125] (Anderson, 2006, p. 26)

wound of Platt's upper right thigh. A fourth bullet (from either Dove or Orrantia) scraped across his back causing an abrasion.

After exiting the Monte Carlo, Platt again shot at McNeill and Mireles. Both agents went down. McNeill took a shot to his neck that rendered him out of the fight and parallelized for several hours. Platt then rushed the agents located behind the Monte Carlo. Agent John Hanlon had joined Dove and Grogan taking a position at the rear of the Grogan/Dove car. All three agents were shot and went to the ground. Platt shot Dove and Grogan at point blank range, killing both agents. Hanlon was shot in the hand and groin, taking him out of the fight (see figure 7-2).

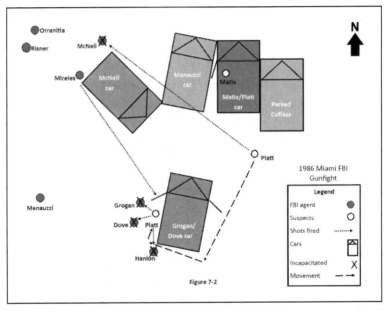

Figure 7-2

Unbelievably, Matix regained consciousness, exited the Monte Carlo and joined Platt at the Grogan/Dove car. Although Mireles was seriously injured, he worked the pump-action shotgun with one hand and was able to shoot at Platt from a sitting position behind McNeill's car. Platt took several hits from the buckshot, but continued to move and get into the driver's seat of the Grogan/Dove car. Matix got into the passenger seat. Platt, with an injured right arm attempted to start the car with his left hand, while Mireles continued to fire the shotgun until it was empty. Pulling himself up, Mireles, drew his Smith and Wesson .357 magnum—loaded with six rounds of .38 +P—and staggered towards the car with the suspects inside. Mireles shot all six rounds into the car hitting Platt once in the head and once in the chest, and Matix three times in the head. With both suspects finally incapacitated, the gunfight was over (see figure 7-3).

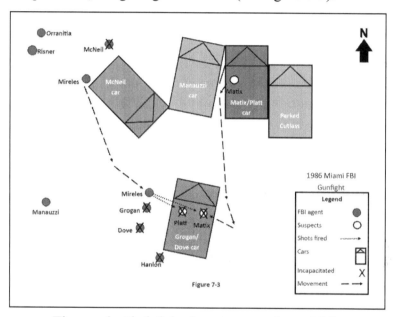

Figure 7-3

The gun battle left both suspects and two FBI agents (Grogan and Dove) dead. Agents Mireles, McNeill, and Hanlon sustained serious injuries. Agents Manauzzi and Orrantia received minor injuries. Agent Risner survived unscathed. There were 49 verified shots fired by the suspects and 70 verified shots by the agents.[126] During the gunfight

---

[126] (Anderson, 2006, p. 13)

Platt received 12 gunshot wounds and Matix six. For a detailed account of the shooting see *Forensic Analysis of the April 11, 1986, FBI Firefight* by Dr. W. French Anderson.

This Miami FBI shooting has been analyzed and scrutinized by federal, state, local, and private police trainers. While there's a lot to be learned about how much trauma a human could take and remain in the fight, one of the biggest outcomes directly associated with this gunfight was the development of the .40 caliber bullet. As in the Newhall shooting, the FBI agents were out gunned by the felons.

The weapons used by the suspects are as follows: Matix was armed with a 12 gauge shotgun (1 round fired). Platt used a .223 caliber rifle (42 rounds fired) and two .357 magnum revolvers (3 rounds fired from each gun). Seven of the eight FBI agents on scene fired shots. The agents were armed as follows: McNeill (6 rounds fired) and Orrantia (12 rounds fired) each had a .357 magnum revolvers loaded with 38+P; Mireles used a 12-gauge shotgun loaded with 00 buckshot (5 rounds fired) and a .357 magnum revolver loaded with 38+P (6 rounds fired); Grogan (9 rounds fired), Dove (20 rounds fired), and Risner (at least 13-14 rounds fired) all used 9mm semi-automatics loaded with 115 grain jacketed hollow point bullets. Risner also fired one round from a .38 revolver loaded with .38 +P. Hanlon (5 rounds fired) used a .38 revolver loaded with .38 +P.[127]

The two largest issues coming out of the incident were (1) Platt inflicted devastating wounds with his rifle; and (2) despite receiving several gunshot wounds, some even fatal, both suspects were able to remain in the fight for several minutes. Following this shooting officers began to doubt their equipment and question the effectiveness of the 9mm bullet to stop an aggressor. The fact is, you must not only be trained and prepared to use your equipment, you must also

---

[127] (Anderson, 2006, p. 13)

be confident *in* your equipment. For years the Fram® company marketed their more expensive oil filters by claiming the quality of protection was worth the price. The tagline for their commercials was, "You can pay me now, or pay me later." Quality does make a difference—especially when it comes to handguns, holsters, and ammunition. However, as with most things, quality doesn't mean the most expensive. Remember, your goal in a gunfight isn't to kill, but to stop the aggressor from killing or attempting to kill. Therefore, you want equipment best suited for stopping quickly and effectively.

Ammunition

Enormous improvement in ballistics has been made since the FBI shooting. This is especially important since the most critical piece of equipment in a gunfight is the bullet. The bullet, which comes in different sizes and weights, is the projectile that comes out of the barrel. The terms "cartridge" and "round" refer collectively to the bullet, case, primer, and gunpowder. Short of the aggressor giving up, it's the bullet that does the stopping.

The effectiveness of a bullet depends on the transfer of kinetic energy from the moving bullet to the object hit by the bullet. The speed or velocity of the bullet determines its kinetic energy. The faster the bullet, the more energy it has available to transfer. A car traveling 70 mph is going to do more damage than the same car traveling 5 mph. The same is true with bullets. It's not the bullet itself, it's the energy of the bullet that's created by its speed. Kinetic energy is proportional to the square of its velocity.[128] Kinetic energy is created by the motion of an object, so the faster the speed the more kinetic energy. That's why the lighter 55 to 77 grain rifle bullets shot from Platt's .223 caliber rifle were far more

---

[128] (The Physics Classroom, 1996-2015)

devastating than the 9mm 115 grain pistol bullets that hit Platt. The muzzle velocity[129] of bullets from the .223 rifle was over 3,000 feet per second (fps). Whereas the 9mm bullets were traveling about 1,200 fps and the .38 +P 900 fps or less.

Velocity is more critical to kinetic energy than mass. However, mass does make a difference. A twenty-pound sledge hammer is going to do a lot more damage than a twelve-ounce finishing hammer traveling at the same speed. Using a large and fast bullet will create more kinetic energy (mass times velocity squared: $KE = mv^2$). Nevertheless, speed is more important than mass.

However, speed can be overdone. Too much speed will result in over penetration. The faster the bullet moves the more likely it will be to completely penetrate the target. This means the bullet passes into and then through its intended target. Over penetration is negative for two reasons: first, a bullet that completely penetrates a target will continue until stopped by something or someone else. Newton's first law of motion: an object in motion will remain in motion until an external force acts upon it. Second, a bullet that completely penetrates a target still has energy and any energy that isn't used to stop the aggressor is wasted energy.

Hollow point bullets were developed in an effort to prevent over penetration. If the bullet doesn't over penetrate means all of its kinetic energy is transferred to the object hit. Bullets are generally made out of lead, because of lead's mass and softness. Full metal jacketed bullets are (generally) lead bullets covered with a thin coat of copper. Hollow point bullets have a hole in the tip. When a hollow point bullet enters an object (i.e. a human body) the bullet is designed to open up and spread out in a mushroom shape, thus slowing it down like a parachute on the back of a drag racer.

---

[129] Muzzle velocity is the speed of the bullet immediately after leaving the gun barrel.

Bullets fragmenting and breaking up also causes loss of effectiveness, especially if the bullet first travels through an object such as a door or glass. This was an issue in the Miami shooting. Several of the bullets recovered from Platt and Matix were fragments.[130] Bullets can also fragment after entering the body. In an effort to keep bullets in one piece, some bullet manufacturers have started bonding the outer jacket to the bullet's core. These are referred to as "bonded" bullets.

While there have been great advances in ballistics, be cautioned, there is no "magic" bullet that's guaranteed to stop a person immediately. What's the best bullet to use? First, let me caution what not to use. Never use hand-loaded ammunition (rounds that are loaded by private individuals) for "duty" ammunition. Even when using the best hand-loaded rounds there is simply too much room for error. Furthermore, in the event of a shooting the decision to use hand-loaded ammunition may have to be defended in court. Hence, the best choice is to use the same rounds used by law enforcement. Ammunition companies manufacture cartridges specifically for law enforcement. Most police agencies do extensive studies prior to selecting ammunition. Check with local and state police agencies for their choice of ammunition. If the question comes up in court concerning the choice of ammunition you may confidently reply that it was based on what police in your area use. Police are the professionals, let them do the research and defend the selection.

As mentioned before, the most effective bullet is the fastest and biggest. Does that mean a 350 grain .500 S&W magnum traveling in excess of 1900 fps is the best choice? No, the law of diminishing returns begins to take effect. Too fast and too big will have too much penetration and will most

---

[130] (Anderson, 2006, pp. 19-76)

likely over penetrate. Also, there's the consideration of practicality. Bigger and faster means a larger cartridge and will require a larger gun. Also, the more powerful the cartridge the bigger the recoil.

The most common calibers used by police are 9mm, .40 S&W, and .45 ACP. Ballistics for the 9mm have developed greatly in recent years. Each of these calibers are proven effective in stopping aggressors. See the chart (figure 7-4) comparing the 9mm, .40 S&W, and .45 ACP. The advantages of the 9mm are its low recoil and smaller cartridges. Low recoil means it's easier to shoot and more manageable, while small cartridges means more ammunition available. The disadvantage is the ballistic capabilities of this round is significantly less in foot pounds than the other two. While it is moving faster than the .45, its mass is much less. The .40 S&W has the best ballistics; the velocity equals the 9mm but it is 41 grains heavier. While larger than the 9mm (less rounds available), it is still smaller than the .45 ACP. The drawback to the .40 S&W is the recoil. Of the three calibers it has the most "kick" when shot. The .45 ACP is the bullet with the most mass, but is traveling the slowest. A general recommendation and popular choice by police for any of these calibers is the Gold Dot® by Speer®.

Speer® Gold Dot® Ammunition			
Caliber	**Weight**	**MV**	**Energy**
9mm	124	1150	364
.40 S&W	165	1150	484
.45 ACP	185	1050	453

Weight: grains
MV: Muzzle Velocity fps
Energy: in foot pounds
(Source: speer-ammo.com/ballistics/ammo.aspx)
Figure 7-4

All three of the above rounds are designed for semi-automatic handguns (although they may be used in specially designed revolvers). If considering a revolver the two most popular calibers are the .38 Special and the .357 Magnum. In the Miami shooting three FBI

Speer® Gold Dot® Ammunition			
Caliber	**Weight**	**MV**	**Energy**
.38+P	125	945	248
.357 Mag.	125	1450	584
.44 Mag.	210	1450	980

Weight: grains
MV: Muzzle Velocity fps
Energy: in foot pounds
(Source: speer-ammo.com/ballistics/ammo.aspx)
Figure 7-5

agents had .357 magnums, but they were loaded with a much less powerful .38+P. Note the difference in energy between the two bullets of the same weight in figure 7-5. Included in the comparison is the .44 Magnum.

Firearms

There are a myriad of quality handguns available in today's market for a variety of purposes. Handguns are designed to meet the specific and very different wants of shooting enthusiasts. There are handguns designed for plinking (targets that pop visually or audibly when hit, like tin cans or glass bottles), competition (from speed shooting to cowboy action shooting to silhouette target shooting), hunting, concealed carry, self-defense, and combat to name a few. With so many different choices, selecting a handgun for the novice shooter can be overwhelming. However, with a little information, you can quickly narrow down the selection.

Choosing a handgun, like any tool, begins with determining its purpose. Select a handgun designed for the specific application for which the gun will be used. A combat handgun will best meet the needs for members of an armed

Safety Response Team. Combat handguns fall into two basic categories: revolver and semi-automatic. Both have benefits. The bottom line is this–anyone involved in a gunfight wants to have the most powerful gun with the most bullets. Realistically, select a handgun that you can safely and accurately shoot and can be carried comfortably concealed (assuming the SRT will be carrying concealed handguns).

Revolvers

The National Rifle Association (NRA) defines a revolver as a handgun "that has a rotating cylinder containing a number of firing chambers. The action of the trigger or hammer will line up a chamber with the barrel and firing pin."[131] There are two basic types of revolvers: single-action and double-action. A single-action revolver is the old "cowboy" style that requires the hammer to be thumbed back to cock the gun. Once cocked the trigger is pulled to release the hammer and fire the gun. With the hammer cocked it doesn't take much pressure on the trigger to release the hammer, causing the gun to fire. Single action revolvers are great for plinking, hunting, or shooting in competitions such as silhouette and Cowboy Action Shooting. A single-action revolver is not recommended, and in fact, highly discouraged for self-defense and combat situations. If opting for a revolver, select a double-action revolver.

Three of the largest American gun companies (Smith and Wesson, Colt, and Ruger) all manufacture quality double-action combat revolvers and smaller revolvers made for concealed carry. Unlike a single-action revolver, the hammer on a double-action revolver doesn't need to be cocked first. When the trigger is pulled the hammer cocks and then drops, causing the gun to fire. The benefit of a double-action/combat revolver over a semi-automatic is its simplicity.

---

[131] (Basic Pistol Course, Natiional Rifle Association, 2009, p. I-3)

Revolvers are easy to learn to shoot, reliable, and rarely have malfunctions. The drawbacks are a limited number of rounds (five or six), the size and weight of full frame guns, and difficulty reloading quickly in high stress situations.

Semi-automatics

Revolvers, as good and reliable as they are, are yesterday's combat guns. Today's combat guns are semi-automatic, double-action only, striker-fire pistols. The world of handguns changed when Sam Colt invented the revolver in 1836. The next major change came when John Browning designed the .45 Automatic Pistol that was manufactured by Colt® and became known as the "1911". The 1911 pistol was issued by the US Army from 1911 to 1986, and remains a popular pistol for self-defense and sport shooting. In 1981 Austrian engineer Gaston Glock developed his "Safe Action"® pistol for the Austrian army. Catching the eye of American police, Glock's double-action only, striker-fire pistol soon became the new standard for combat pistols. As with double-action revolvers and model 1911 pistols, today nearly every major gun company makes a double-action only, striker-fire pistol.

Like single-action revolvers, single-action semi-automatic pistols perform a single action when the trigger is pulled. The drawback of single-action semi-automatic pistols (such as the 1911) is the same as single-action revolvers; they traditionally have a short and rather light trigger pull that may lead to unintentional discharges in high stress situations. They also have a positive safety that must be disengaged prior to firing. Hence, in high stress situations you must remember to disengage the safety. Unless you've trained enough to create a reflexive response to disengaging the safety, chances are you will find yourself trying to discharge a locked weapon in a deadly gunfight.

The double-action only semi-automatics mimic the trigger pull of a double-action revolver, albeit with a shorter trigger pull. For police officers of the 1980s and 1990s, who were transitioning from a revolver to a semi-automatic, the double-action semi-automatic was more natural and required less training. In 1992, after carrying a Smith and Wesson revolver as a duty gun since 1979 (in both the Air Force and on the department), the San Antonio Police Department switched me to the Glock model 22. The transition from a revolver to the Glock pistol took three training days with about 700 rounds fired. In 2009 I joined the Bonneville County Sheriff's Office as a reserve deputy and was issued a Para Ordinance 1911. I had to relearn the reflexive response of disengaging a manual safety—something I had not done since the beginning of my law enforcement career. I repeatedly forgot to disengage the slide lock safety at the beginning of each shooting stage when given the command to fire. I had a tough time readjusting to the 1911, but the key is training. Remember, the more complicated the tool, the more training and repetition required.

Finally, keep in mind that whatever handgun you select, you should always ensure it is designed for combat and you must train with it to obtain a solid level of competence.

Firearm modifications

If it can be attached to a gun, labeled "tactical" and painted OD green or black it will sell in the world of firearms. The firearms industry has an ever-increasing list of accessories to modify, enhance, or add-on to handguns. The manufactures attempt to make the consumer believe the gun isn't good enough right out of the box. In order to be a better shot attachments must be added, triggers must be modified, and sights must be replaced—hogwash! That just doesn't fly in the world of combat. Perhaps this is true in handgun competitions or hunting, but in the world of combat quality handguns come ready for action. There's simply too much at stake for gun companies not to produce an out-of-the-box ready gun. Police departments purchase combat handguns by the hundreds or thousands and they expect them to be dependable with no modifications necessary—and they are.

Keep your carry firearm as simple and as close to factory specifications as possible. Most police departments forbid officers to modify their service pistols. Those that do permit alterations require that a certified armorer perform the modifications. The most important piece of equipment in a gunfight is your brain, but the second is your gun. You want it to be reliable and consistent. Your firearm becomes increasingly more complicated with the addition of modifications or special equipment. Plus, each addition carries its own set of uncontrollable factors like malfunction or user error.

That being said, there are some acceptable and popular modifications to a combat handgun such as sights, lighting systems, and grips. All combat handguns come equipped with their own sights. These are often referred to as the gun's iron sights. However, iron sights are regularly replaced by night sights. In fact, many police departments order their duty pistols with night sights from the manufacturer. Night sights are designed to provide greater sight visibility in low light situations. Generally, this modification uses a three-dot system with two dots inset in the rear sight and one dot inset in the front sight. These dots have radioactive isotopes that cause them to "glow" in low and no-light environments. Trijicon® makes night sights for all popular combat pistols. They run about $125 for a set plus the necessary cost of a gunsmith mounting them. Besides night sights, laser sights are an acceptable and popular modification. They even come standard on some of today's pistols. However, laser sights should never be used to teach someone how to shoot. Laser sights should only supplement a proper sight picture. Under high stress conditions it's easier to pick up your firearm's front sight than to look for a small laser bouncing around off a moving and mobile target. Because of this, laser sights should not be relied upon for combat use. Perhaps the best aftermarket optics becoming popular today are see-through, low-profile, micro reflex sights that allow the shooter to use either enhanced optics or the gun's iron sights. The pricey, but quality Smith and Wesson® M&P C.O.R.E (Competition Optics Ready Equipment) 9mm comes ready for mounting one of these high-priced optics. This modification could very well be the wave of the future for police.

Lighting systems are the other acceptable and popular addition. This modification places a small, tactical use only light onto your firearm. Where the laser sight provides bullet placement precision, the gun-mounted light provides whole target illumination. However, a gun-mounted light should only be supplemental to a hand-held flashlight. There's too big a temptation to use the gun as a flashlight. Recall the second cardinal rule of firearms safety—*never point your muzzle at anything you're not willing to destroy*. Therefore, if an SRT trains with lights I recommend becoming skilled using handheld flashlights and only use gun-mounted lights as supplements when the gun will be pointed exclusively at the threat.

Finally, aftermarket grips for some models are also popular and easy to install. Grips of various sizes and textures are available. Larger or smaller grips will help you to have a proper and consistent hold on the gun. Rubberized grips can provide a more secure hold and comfortable fit and thereby decrease the chances of hand fatigue. However, avoid grips, holsters, or any other add-on item that features images or writing that may be misinterpreted by a jury. Remember, in the event of a shooting, your handgun will be confiscated for evidence and presented to the jury in the event of a trial. You probably don't want to have a skull and crossbones, the "Grim Reaper" or "Zombie Hunter" etched into the side of your gun.

Holsters

Every handgun should be carried in a holster that is specifically designed for that handgun. The holster should protect the trigger from being unintentionally pulled and should securely hold the handgun in place. Just like selecting a gun, you must think about combat when selecting a holster. A good combat holster will allow you to have a proper grip while the gun is still holstered. It must be both safe and comfortable. If the holster is uncomfortable or causes fatigue, then you might be tempted to carry without it. I highly discourage anyone from carrying a gun without a good quality holster designed specifically for their firearm. Many people like to carry a handgun in their waistband, inside a tucked-in shirt. While concealed and secure, this makes it difficult to draw and quickly get into a gunfight. Although it may feel secure, and it does conceal your weapon, it is a dangerous practice. You are far more likely to accidentally discharge your firearm without proper trigger protection. Also, holsters secure your firearm to your body so they do not slip or shift. This makes gripping and handling them far safer in the event of a genuine threat.

Many holsters are made from soft nylon material and are designed simply to carry a handgun securely and safely; but they are not designed to draw from in a combat situation. Other holsters are competition holsters designed specifically for quick draw, but lack safety features. Holsters made from leather are good, but need to be "broken in" and stretch over time. Fobus® and Blackhawk® make quality combat holsters designed specifically for plain clothes or concealed carry. These holsters are made from durable molded material that secures the gun and allows for a quick draw.

Radios

Your SRTs will need more than just firearms and holsters to adequately protect your parish, congregation or synagogue. Both armed and unarmed SRTs will benefit from the use of quality, two-way handheld radios. Technology has driven down their cost, and quality radios are available with whisper microphones and earbuds for a reasonable price at most sporting goods stores. You can find a large, budget-friendly selection by searching for radios used in hunting. Of course, if budget allows, higher-end radios that are much more secure are available. If radios are issued to your team make sure training includes their use. Every member of an armed SRT should practice wearing and using a radio on the side opposite their gun is carried. Training should also include releasing the radio and grasping the gun so that your reflexive response in a real gunfight will allow you to address the first priority—stopping a shooter.

Identification badges

Many church safety teams issue identification badges for team members. These can be as prominent or discreet as desired. Badges may be as simple as name tags with different colors, distinguishing between ushers, unarmed SRT members and armed SRT members. Only those privy to the meaning of the different colors will know the difference. Churches may also chose not to have any identification badges or name tags for SRT members. Two theories drive the opposing viewpoints. For those who believe the teams' identity and purpose should easily be identified also believe it serves as a sense of security to the congregation and guests and a warning to those who may consider disrupting the service. Sometimes something as simple as a name tag is regarded as a sign of authority and may help deescalate a disturbance.

On the other hand, some believe identifying the teams publically may create unnecessary fear and needlessly identify to an aggressor those who will offer resistance. A compromise is to place signs indicating there is an armed Safety Response Team on duty without identifying team members. Church leadership will have to make the decision they believe will best provide safety to their congregation and guests. Some church leaders feel it is best not to publically announce an armed team is in place. Again, this will vary from church to church and depend on the government and size of the church. Smaller and congregational led churches have a greater responsibility to inform the membership of decisions by leadership. Also, leaders need to consider training their congregation on how to respond in the event of an active shooter. Keep in mind there will likely be those in the congregation who carry concealed at church. While these law-abiding citizens aren't there to harm innocent people, in the event of a gunfight they may not know there are good guys with guns trained to respond.

General Security Concerns
Chapter 8

Charleston Church Massacre

On Wednesday evenings a small group of parishioners routinely gathered at Emmanuel AME Church in Charleston, South Carolina, for prayer and a Bible study. On June, 17, 2015, the African American parishioners were joined by a young white man, 21-year old Dylann Roof. Roof arrived at about 8 pm and was welcomed into the small group of twelve. An hour later Roof stood and announced that he was there to kill black people. Pulling a semi-automatic pistol from his backpack, Roof started shooting. He fatally wounded nine people. The church's pastor Rev. Clementa Pinckney was among the dead. One witness said the assailant reloaded as many as five times during the assault. Roof fled but was arrested the next day in North Carolina.[132]

At the end of each year President and CEO of Lifeway Christian Resources, Thom Rainer, gives his predictions of popular trends American churches will face in the coming year. No doubt, the Charleston massacre was one of

---

[132] (Ellis, Payne, Perez, & Ford, 2015)

149

the reasons that Rainer predicted the number one trend for 2016 will be an accelerated growth in church security ministries. Rainer writes, "Shootings in churches and sex abuse of children mandate this unfortunate trend. No church can afford to be without serious security measures, policies, and equipment. It will evolve into a major church ministry."[133]

It remains incumbent upon each church to review security issues and shore-up areas that need attention regardless of their decision on implementing an armed Safety Response Team. Available resources to help evaluate security concerns include church insurance companies, local law enforcement officers, and federal agencies. Many insurance companies are proactive and provide information and recommendations for security, including the use of armed security teams. Various law enforcement agencies have resource officers available to provide free security assessments of your facilities. The Department of Homeland Security has information about responding to active-shooter events on their website (See: http://www.dhs.gov/active-shooter-preparedness).

Thinking about security issues can be overwhelming. Where do you start? A systematic approach is perhaps best, starting with human threats from outside of your facility and congregation and working to the inside. Begin with the big picture and move to small snap shots. Stay focused on one type of threat at a time; this book focuses on active-shooter events, which is a good starting point. Active-shooter events are those situations in which a person(s) is actively engaged in murdering parishioners, guests, or staff on church property. Proper preparation for an active killer will also help prevent or deter other threats (e.g. preparing for an active shooter will also help secure against burglary and robbery). However, remain focused on one threat at a time as you review and prepare security procedures.

---

[133] (Rainer, 2015)

Human threats

Begin the assessment by looking at potential human threats that exist right now. Human threats can come from outside or inside the congregation. First, consider human threats from outside your congregation. Are there any potential threats in your community? Are there emotionally charged issues that may send someone "over the edge" and attack a house of worship where you live? Does your church hold any positions that activist groups are attacking? While we don't need to be paranoid we also don't want to bury our heads in the sand. Remember, Nehemiah remained in Condition Yellow (aware and ready for action) as he endeavored the unpopular rebuilding of the walls around Jerusalem. Churches that proclaim the gospel and stand for biblical principles will always draw objection by some people in the community. And a few will be filled with rage and perhaps turn to violence. However, it may not only be a rage fueled by hate for the church's positions or what it symbolizes. Unfortunately, it may be the rage of someone inside your congregation.

Don't ignore a disgruntled member, scorned spouse, disillusioned guest, or distraught neighbor. In the majority of active-shooter events, the killer had a previous connection with those he targeted.[134] The following is a description of active shooter characteristics provided by law enforcement:

- Active shooters usually intend their actions to be an expression of hatred or rage, rather than financial gain or motives associated with other types of crimes.

---

[134] (Federal Bureau of Investigation, Critical Incident Response Group, n.d.)

- Active shooters often, but not always, are suicidal. Escape from the police is often not a priority of an active shooter. Most active shooters have not attempted to hide their identity.
- Active shooters make detailed plans for the attack. Often they are better armed than the police. They usually have some familiarity with the chosen location. In some cases they have planned diversions or booby traps, such as explosives.
- In some situations, active shooters chose a location for tactical advantage, such as a high, protected location. In other incidents, active shooters have remained mobile.[135]

Making a mental note of possible threats is not enough. As I said before, a systematic approach will provide the best results. And since intelligence collection is critical in identifying potential threats, either from outside or inside the congregation, you will want to systematically approach this concept as well. Collecting intelligence is generally little more than: encouraging parishioners to report possible or actual threats; keeping your eyes and ears open to what is going on in your community and church; recording the information; and sharing it with team members. A record of information collected should then be kept in a secure location and retained until the threat is over.

Geographical location

Think about the geographical location of your facility(ies). Are you located downtown or in a rural or urban

---

[135] (Police Executive Research Forum, 2014, p. 9)

neighborhood? Is your building(s) on a major thoroughfare or tucked away in a neighborhood? How long will it take law enforcement to respond? Bear in mind that Sunday mornings, when most churches meet for worship, are generally when the fewest patrol officers are on duty. Furthermore, other typical days and times worshippers may meet (i.e. Saturday mornings or evenings), law enforcement is also spread thin or busy responding to calls for service. Finally, the availability of "back-up" officers who are not first responders (i.e. detectives, trainers, and administrative staff) are usually off on weekends.

Parking lot

Other than collecting information in advance and putting a stop to an aggressor long before he steps on your property, the parking lot is generally the earliest place to recognize and engage a threat. If a potential attacker is spotted in the parking lot (i.e. a man carrying a rifle is walking toward the entrance), lockdown procedures should be implemented and law enforcement notified. Lockdown procedures include locking all doors and the congregation staying in or going to a designated area. If the threat is locked outside the facilities, everyone should gather in an inner room, away from exterior doors and windows. If the room has exterior doors and windows, pull the shades and keep people away from doors and windows where they can be targeted from outside; bullets easily penetrate window glass and most doors. If your secure room has windows but no shades, blinds, or curtains that can be easily and quickly closed to prevent someone outside from seeing in, then consider installing some.

If feasible, an assailant locked out should be kept under constant surveillance while someone remains in contact with the police dispatcher. If the gunman leaves the property, provide the dispatcher a description of the suspect, what he is wearing, his weapon(s), means of escape (e.g. foot, vehicle) and the direction of travel. While the aggressor remains outside the armed SRT members should take positions of cover and/or concealment inside the church building, allowing them to confront the gunman from cover and/or concealment in the event he attempts to force his way inside.

Recognizing a threat in the parking lot necessitates designating someone to watch the parking lot as people arrive. It's a good idea to have a team member assigned as that designated person. Along with the parking lot, don't overlook other places an assailant may hide. Possible hiding places include inside or behind storage buildings, fences, bushes or other foliage. Look for any place a person can conceal himself for a short period while he waits for the opportune time to attack. A quick walk around the property before each service may be in order.

Foyer

In most houses of worship there's a foyer or lobby area between the main entrance and the doors leading to the worship center or sanctuary. It's a good idea to have a team member positioned in this area watching people enter the foyer from the outside. While some of these lobby areas may be quite large, usually they are small compared to the main worship area. The confined quarters of a foyer provide a better opportunity to contain and stop an aggressor before he launches an attack in the sanctuary. You may be able to force him back outside—protecting people gathered in the sanctuary. The team member assigned to the lobby should be positioned near the interior doors leading into the worship area. If a would-be-assailant enters the foyer, try to engage and stop him or force him to retreat back outside the building. By placing yourself between an aggressor and the sanctuary you are giving him an escape route away from potential victims. Don't make his only option the sanctuary or another area you don't want him to go (i.e. classrooms or nursery). If you are able to force him back outside go into lockdown procedures.

Doors

Most church entrance doors are made to be welcoming with some additional security against inclement weather and perhaps burglary when the building is vacant. The fact is, church doors provide more aesthetic appeal and protection from the elements than physical security or protection from an assailant. As the weather permits (or perhaps demands), many churches open their doors to the fresh air. Even if they had the money, few churches want to exchange existing entrance doors for expensive high security doors (some churches in high crime areas already have these in place). An armed SRT team will have to work with what's in place at their house of worship.

Some questions to ask are: Can the doors be easily and quickly locked to keep out an aggressor, or at least slow him down substantially? Who has keys or access? Can someone easily gain access before services begin and hide until he decides to attack? When are the doors unlocked and locked? Locking the doors (either all doors or all but one) after the service begins may be an option, if someone is available to open the doors and welcome late arrivers. Are there other entrance doors, not normally used, but unlocked when services are being held? If so, think about locking these, requiring everyone without a key to use the main entrance.

Interior doors leading from the foyer or lobby into the worship center should be closed once the service begins. This will at least force an assailant to open the door, occupying one hand, and hopefully alerting a team member and the pastor or worship leader. Many churches have side doors that lead into the worship center or backstage. These doors

155

should be locked unless it is necessary for them to be unlocked. In large churches that have more than one main entrance, there will likely be sufficient team members to monitor traffic in and out of those doors.

In recent years, interior doors (especially classroom and nursery doors) have been modified by eliminating locks and installing windows. These modifications are intended to discourage inappropriate behavior by child predators. However, in an active-shooter event it is best for teachers and nursery workers to have the ability to lock the doors keeping a killer from finding more victims. This may mean reinstalling locks and blinds or shades that can be pulled to prevent someone from seeing inside the room.

Other onsite facilities should also be assessed. Separate buildings used for Sunday school or other classes before, during, or after the worship service should be kept locked. These facilities should only be unlocked as people arrive for class. Shortly after classes begin, lock the doors. If no one is available to monitor late arrivals, install doorbells and instruct a teacher or another responsible adult only to allow entrance to people they trust—just like at home.

Team placement

The physical placement of armed Safety Response Team members is critical to effectively respond to an assailant. If available, prior to the service one member should be positioned outside to monitor people arriving. A second should be positioned in the foyer or lobby, and a third in the main worship area. If only two team members are available then one should be outside and the second in the foyer. If only one member is available then the best location is likely the foyer position. The foyer or lobby position should provide the best surveillance to stop an aggressor entering into the building or engaging an assailant who is already inside.

After the service begins SRT members should be staggered around the worship center, not bunched together. Team members should sit in an aisle seat so they can confront an aggressor with as little interference from congregants as possible. Scenario training will help reveal where team members should be placed. Try to maintain a tactical position and avoid crossfire.

Perhaps the most critical (and vulnerable) position is inside the sanctuary next to the primary entrance. Determine the most likely door an aggressor will enter and place an armed SRT member at that location. He or she can be standing or sitting; this is the first and primary defender.

Video

Technology has driven down the price of video equipment and made it easier than ever before to install, operate, and monitor. That being said, churches use video primarily for recording and not real-time video monitoring. In order to use video to foil an imminent active-shooter attack it must be monitored in real-time by a member of the armed SRT from a safe location that provides cover for an immediate response, or allows the SRT member to contact a team member via a two-way radio. Wi-Fi technology allows video to be monitored from virtually anywhere in real-time on a tablet or smartphone.

Using multiple video cameras allows two or more areas to be monitored by one person. But, the person must be attentive and make sure the cameras are working properly. Cameras can be a false sense of security. Cameras are mechanical devices that malfunction from time to time. Therefore, ensure a backup plan is in place for use during equipment failure.

Congregational drills

Just like an armed SRT needs training, the congregation should also be trained on how to respond to an active-shooter event. As discussed, the natural response to interpersonal human aggression is flight, fight, or fright. The chances of a proper response are greatly increased by informing parishioners of what to expect and training them on how to respond. Just like fire drills, the Federal Emergency Management Agency (FEMA) recommends active-shooter drills:

> The house of worship's EOP [Emergency Operating Procedure] should include courses of action that will describe how congregants and staff can most effectively respond to an active-shooter situation to minimize the loss of life, and teach and train on these practices.
>
> Law enforcement officers may not be present when a shooting begins. Providing information on how congregants and staff can respond to the incident can help prevent and reduce the loss of life.
>
> No single response fits all active-shooter situations; however, making sure each individual knows his or her options for response and can react decisively will save valuable time. Depicting scenarios and considering response options in advance will assist individuals and groups in quickly selecting their best course of action.[136]

---

[136] (Federal Emergency Management Agency, 2013, p. 28)

With an armed SRT in place, the goal is to have the congregation out of the line of fire. Armed SRT members need to engage the aggressor quickly and effectively. With the congregation down and out of the way, the SRT will be able to engage safer and faster.

After the SRT is trained and ready, church leadership should inform the congregation what is expected of them. If an aggressor enters the worship center the congregants should immediately drop to the floor while the SRT stands, moves toward, and engages the assailant. The signal for the congregation should come from the person leading the service at the time (normally this is the pastor or worship leader). By going through some simple drills the congregation can easily learn the proper response.

Anyone regularly up front should train with the armed SRT during the force-on-force scenario training. If a gun or knife wielding aggressor enters the sanctuary the pastor or other leader needs to yell, "Gun!" or "Knife!" while pointing at the assailant. However, anyone can sound the alarm. The important point is that the congregants get to the ground. Rather than panic and freeze, training drills seek to condition congregations to go to the floor for concealment as the SRT engages the assailant. These actions are intended to cause the aggressor to pause and focus on the up-front leader and/or those coming at him. An aggressive response by a church will likely come as a surprise and cause the assailant to hesitate—giving the SRT a tactical advantage.

Conclusion

Implementing Safety Response Teams should not cause panic, but provide real safety and comfort to those attending houses of worship. A proper approach is a balanced approach. We must remember the lesson from Nehemiah, *"And we prayed to our God and set a guard as a protection against them day and night"* (Neh. 4:9). Faith in God and taking personal responsibility is a balanced approach.

Shortly after the Charleston massacre Mayor Joe Riley commented, "People in prayer Wednesday evening. A ritual, a coming together, praying, worshiping God. An awful person to come in and shoot them is inexplicable."[137] Inexplicable. Unfathomable. Incomprehensible. All words that describe the phenomena of armed assailants gunning down innocent people gathered for worship in America. A new America that is changing before our eyes. But here's another word: *Reality*. This is a real threat to American churches.

On February 6, 2016, the *Detroit News* reported Khalil Abu-Rayyan, 21, had been arrested by federal law enforcement officers after telling undercover FBI operatives that he had planned to "shoot up" a church in Detroit. The FBI reported the Michigan man is a supporter of the Islamic State of Iran and Syria, known as ISIS or ISIL. According to the media report, the federal complaint read,

> [R]egarding increasingly violent threats he [Abu-Rayyan] has made to others about committing acts of terror and martyrdom — including brutal acts against police officers, churchgoers and others — on behalf of the foreign terrorist organization Islamic State of Iraq and Levant.[138]

Here are the chilling words of the would-be-assailant reported to undercover FBI employees concerning his plans:

> I tried to shoot up a church one day. I don't know the name of it, but it's close to my job. It's one of the biggest ones in Detroit. Ya[eh],

---

[137] (Ellis, Payne, Perez, & Ford, 2015)
[138] (Hicks, 2016)

I had it planned out. I bought a bunch of bullets. I practiced a lot with it. I practiced reloading and unloading. But my dad searched my car one day, and he found everything. He found the gun and the bullets and a mask I was going to wear. A lot of people go there. Plus people are not allowed to carry guns in church. Plus it would make the news. Everybody would've heard. Honestly I regret not doing it. (If I) can't go do jihad at the Middle East, I would do my jihad over here.

When fire threated our churches we responded. When child predators threatened our churches we responded. When gun-wielding assailants threaten our churches, will we respond?

Faith in God and taking personal responsibility is in order. Christians should never lose sight of God's love for every person in the world as demonstrated in the death of his Son on the cross for our sin. Using lethal force against another human being is not to be taken lightly. Protecting innocent life from illegal and unjustified aggression is also not to be taken lightly.

"This is my commandment, that you love one another as I have loved you. Greater love has no one than this, that someone lay down his life for his friends."
(John 15:12-13)

Questions and Objections
Chapter 9

Using deadly force against another human being is a serious issue. The high value Christians place on the sanctity of life causes many believers to question the moral aspects of using lethal force against another human, even when that person is attempting to kill. Emotions run high as Christians search for answers by looking to the Bible and Christian leaders. Jerry Falwell, Jr. (president of Liberty University) and John Piper (chancellor of Bethlehem College & Seminary) are examples of two Christian brothers who hold different views concerning the use of lethal force for self-defense or defense of another person.

Why are Christians divided on such a critical issue? The use of lethal force for self-defense isn't the only issue (nor will it be the last!) about which Christians hold different understandings. Using lethal force is a highly emotional issue and many times those emotions and biases significantly impact how they approach and interpret Scripture. In this chapter I will pointedly address recent questions and/or objections to the use of lethal force by Christians for self-protection or protection of another.

1. **Question or Objection:** Aren't Christians prohibited from retaliating against another? The Bible says vengeance belongs to the Lord.

Repay no one evil for evil, but give thought to do what is honorable in the sight of all. If possible, so far as it depends on you, live peaceably with all. Beloved, never avenge yourselves, but leave it to the wrath of God, for it is written, "Vengeance is mine, I will repay, says the Lord." To the contrary, "if your enemy is hungry, feed him; if he is thirsty, give him something to drink; for by so doing you will heap burning coals on his head." Do not be overcome by evil, but overcome evil with good. (Romans 12:17-21)

Response: Agreed, Christians aren't to seek vengeance and are prohibited from doing so by the Romans 12 text and others. Vengeance (the meting out of justice[139]) does belong to the Lord (also see Lev. 19:18; 1 Sam. 20:16; Nah. 1:2; Heb. 10:30). However, the Romans 12 text isn't addressing self-defense or defense of another, it's specifically addressing vengeance. Verse 17 begins with the word *repay* meaning to give back to another, to render what is due.[140] Repayment takes place after the threat has passed, not while the threat still exists. For example, if an assailant threw down his gun, raised his hands in surrender, and posed no further threat then to shoot him down would be taking vengeance. This would violate the biblical principle that vengeance belongs to the Lord. In this case the proper response is to ensure he is no longer a threat, secure him and turn him over to the authorities.

2. **Question or Objection:** Aren't Christians to live in peace with all people? Romans 12:18 says to *"live peaceably with all."*

---

[139] (Blue Letter Bible, n.d.)
[140] **Invalid source specified.**

164

Response: No, Christians aren't mandated to live in peace with all people. The entire verse says, *"If possible, so far as it depends on you, live peaceably with all."* The mandate is to live in peace with all, if it is possible—*so far as it depends on you.* Romans 12:18 isn't addressing a response to stop an attack but a prohibition against initiating an attack when unnecessary to maintain or secure peace. The goal is to live in peace with all. Christians are to *seek* peace. But sometimes peace simply isn't possible. There are some people who will initiate a physical attack; their goal is not peace but destruction or annihilation. As stated in chapter two, when an aggressor wielding a gun walks into a church it is not possible to live in peace.

3. **Question or Objection:** Isn't the government responsible for the safety of its citizens? The Bible says the government's authority comes from God and government is the *"avenger who carries out God's wrath on the wrongdoer."*

   Let every person be subject to the governing authorities. For there is no authority except from God, and those that exist have been instituted by God. Therefore whoever resists the authorities resists what God has appointed, and those who resist will incur judgment. For rulers are not a terror to good conduct, but to bad. Would you have no fear of the one who is in authority? Then do what is good, and you will receive his approval, for he is God's servant for your good. But if you do wrong, be afraid, for he does not bear the sword in vain. For he is the servant of God, an avenger who carries out God's wrath on the wrongdoer. (Romans 13:1-4)

165

Response: Yes, the government is responsible for the safety of its citizens. With that responsibility comes authority given by God to carry out the charge as Romans 13:1-4 clearly states. The government has the right to make rules for citizens to live by and to carrying out punishment against those who break the law. The government also has the authority to enforce the law, by physical and lethal force if necessary. In first century Rome the Roman government was the sovereign authority over Jews, but Rome delegated some authority to the Jewish people. The Jewish court had powers of arrest and punishment.

Like ancient Rome, the government of the United States holds the same responsibility and authority to ensure the safety of its citizens. This authority is realized in the criminal justice system made up of federal, state, and local police agencies, courts, jails, and prisons. However, America's founding fathers understood the government is incapable of protecting individual citizens. In fact, the government is even incapable of ensuring the protection of its own president. Four of our presidents were murdered by gun wielding assassins. Several others were shot or shot at—even as recently as 1980 with the failed assassination attempt on President Reagan. Knowing the limitations of the government to protect its citizens the founding fathers gave Americans the authority to protect themselves with the use of firearms in the Second Amendment. The individual states decide the laws concerning citizens carrying firearms in public.

4. **Question or Objection:** Shouldn't Christians expect and accept unjust mistreatment without retaliation? Peter writes in his first letter:

In this you rejoice, though now for a little while, if necessary, you have been grieved by various trials, so that the tested genuineness of your faith—more precious than gold that perishes though it is tested by fire—may be found to result in praise and glory and honor at the revelation of Jesus Christ. (1 Pet. 1:6-7)

Therefore, preparing your minds for action, and being sober-minded, set your hope fully on the grace that will be brought to you at the revelation of Jesus Christ. (1 Pet. 1:13)

For what credit is it if, when you sin and are beaten for it, you endure? But if when you do good and suffer for it you endure, this is a gracious thing in the sight of God. For to this you have been called, because Christ also suffered for you, leaving you an example, so that you might follow in his steps. (1 Pet. 2:20-21)

Response: This question is misleading. There are actually three questions being asked. The first is "Shouldn't Christians *expect* unjust mistreatment?" Yes, Christians should expect unjust treatment; Jesus said we would be persecuted for the sake of the gospel (see Mark 10:30).

The second question is, "Shouldn't Christians *accept* unjust mistreatment?" The answer to this question depends on who is being unjust and what the mistreatment entails. If the mistreatment amounts to verbal insults from family, neighbors, co-workers, or people who just don't like us then the answer is, "Yes, we should accept the unjust mistreatment." However, if the unjust mistreatment is physical assault from family, neighbors, co-workers, or people who just don't like us the answer is, "No, we shouldn't just accept the unjust mistreatment." If the unjust mistreatment is from the government and Christians are being persecuted unjustly *for*

167

their faith, the witness from Scripture is not to resist with physical force against government officials.

The third question is, "Should Christians retaliate against unjust mistreatment?" No, Christians should not respond to unjust mistreatment by retaliating against another who has harmed them. But retaliation and self-defense are separate issues. Self-defense is the immediate response to stop a physical assault or to prevent an imminent physical assault.

5. **Question or Objection:** Isn't the proper Christian response to violent hostility the endurance of suffering and bearing a strong testimony?

> *But before all this they will lay their hands on you and persecute you, delivering you up to the synagogues and prisons, and you will be brought before kings and governors for my name's sake. This will be your opportunity to bear witness. Settle it therefore in your minds not to meditate beforehand how to answer, for I will give you a mouth and wisdom, which none of your adversaries will be able to withstand or contradict. You will be delivered up even by parents and brothers and relatives and friends, and some of you they will put to death. You will be hated by all for my name's sake. But not a hair of your head will perish. By your endurance you will gain your lives.* (Luke 21:12-19)

Response: Once again, the text cited is a reference to government oppression not criminal aggression. Some will also use Matthew 10 to support the premise that Christians are to respond to violent hostility with suffering and testimony, not lethal force. However, in the passages cited

168

the hostility is clearly coming from the government and not individual criminals, street gangs, or terrorist organizations.

6. **Question or Objection:** Aren't Christians significantly hindering the advancement of God's kingdom when they use the sword (or gun)?

   Jesus answered, "My kingdom is not of this world. If my kingdom were of this world, my servants would have been fighting, that I might not be delivered over to the Jews. But my kingdom is not from the world." (John 18:36)

   Then Jesus said to him, "Put your sword back into its place. For all who take the sword will perish by the sword." (Matt. 26:52)

Response: This question continues to conflate self-defense (the action used to protect yourself or another from an illegal and harmful physical attack at the hands of an individual) with the use of militaristic force to carry out vigilante justice. State and federal law support the individual's right to defend against physical harm. The government understands the limitation of police officers to be everywhere at all times for protection.

7. **Question or Objection:** Is using lethal force against another returning evil for evil?

   You have heard that it was said, 'An eye for an eye and a tooth for a tooth.' But I say to you, Do not resist the one who is evil. But if anyone slaps you on the right cheek, turn to him the other also." (Matt. 5:38-19)

169

Response: No, using lethal force to protect life is not returning evil for evil. In fact, I believe it's returning good (the protection of innocent life) for evil (the unlawful harming of innocent life). The proper understanding of this text is discussed in chapter two. In short, Jesus is speaking about retaliation to verbal insults not physical assaults. Jesus was not addressing self-defense.

8. **Question or Objection:** Shouldn't churches in America respond to persecution just like the church in Acts did?

> *[F]or truly in this city there were gathered together against your holy servant Jesus, whom you anointed, both Herod and Pontius Pilate, along with the Gentiles and the peoples of Israel, to do whatever your hand and your plan had predestined to take place. And now, Lord, look upon their threats and grant to your servants to continue to speak your word with all boldness, while you stretch out your hand to heal, and signs and wonders are performed through the name of your holy servant Jesus." And when they had prayed, the place in which they were gathered together was shaken, and they were all filled with the Holy Spirit and continued to speak the word of God with boldness.* (Acts 4:27-31)

> *[A]nd when they had called in the apostles, they beat them and charged them not to speak in the name of Jesus, and let them go. Then they left the presence of the council, rejoicing that they were counted worthy to suffer dishonor for the name.* (Acts 5:40-41)

And Saul approved of his execution. And there arose on that day a great persecution against the church in Jerusalem, and they were all scattered throughout the regions of Judea and Samaria, except the apostles. Devout men buried Stephen and made great lamentation over him. But Saul was ravaging the church, and entering house after house, he dragged off men and women and committed them to prison. (Acts 8:1-3)

Response: Yes, if the state or federal governments were arresting pastors and teachers for preaching the gospel, then there should not be an uprising of arms to shoot officials carrying out the wishes of the government. However, we must remember that the response of the church in Acts was to oppression by governmental authorities against the gospel. In fact, Paul did use his right as a Roman citizen on two occasions in Acts. The first time Paul asserted his right as a Roman citizen was to force the authorities at Philippi to come and personally release him from prison.

But when it was day, the magistrates sent the police, saying, "Let those men go." And the jailer reported these words to Paul, saying, "The magistrates have sent to let you go. Therefore come out now and go in peace." But Paul said to them, "They have beaten us publicly, uncondemned, men who are Roman citizens, and have thrown us into prison; and do they now throw us out secretly? No! Let them come themselves and take us out." The police reported these words to the magistrates, and they were afraid when they heard that they were Roman citizens. So they came

171

and apologized to them. And they took them out and asked them to leave the city. So they went out of the prison and visited Lydia. And when they had seen the brothers, they encouraged them and departed. (Acts 16:35-40)

The second incident in which Paul asserted his rights as a Roman citizen was to spare him from a physical beating.

But when they had stretched him out for the whips, Paul said to the centurion who was standing by, "Is it lawful for you to flog a man who is a Roman citizen and uncondemned?" When the centurion heard this, he went to the tribune and said to him, "What are you about to do? For this man is a Roman citizen." So the tribune came and said to him, "Tell me, are you a Roman citizen?" And he said, "Yes."... So those who were about to examine him withdrew from him immediately, and the tribune also was afraid, for he realized that Paul was a Roman citizen and that he had bound him. (Acts 22:25-29)

The laws in Rome were designed to protect Roman citizens from unjust physical harm and Paul used those laws to his benefit. Citizens in the United States are afforded laws that allow them to use lethal force to protect themselves from unjust physical harm. Using lawful means for self-defense doesn't violate Scripture.

9. **Question or Objection:** Did Jesus really intend for his disciples to buy swords or was he simply speaking metaphorically?

And he said to them, "When I sent you out with no moneybag or knapsack or sandals, did you lack anything?" They said, "Nothing." He said to them, "But now let the one who has a moneybag take it, and likewise a knapsack. And let the one who has no sword sell his cloak and buy one. For I tell you that this Scripture must be fulfilled in me: 'And he was numbered with the transgressors.' For what is written about me has its fulfillment." And they said, "Look, Lord, here are two swords." And he said to them, "It is enough." (Luke 22:35-38)

Response: Yes, it seems he did. Although, the use of lethal force to defend or proclaim the gospel cannot be supported by Scripture. Nevertheless, Jesus did clearly tell his apostles to obtain swords. So the question remains, "What did Jesus mean by telling his apostles to carry swords?" Some believe that Jesus was speaking symbolically and never intended for his disciples to obtain real swords. But in other places where the disciples were confused or mistaken the gospel writers indicate the disciples' misunderstandings. Here are some examples from Luke's gospel:

Then those who were at table with him began to say among themselves, "Who is this, who even forgives sins?" (Luke 7:49)

And when his disciples asked him what this parable meant, he said, "To you it has been given to know the secrets of the kingdom of God, but for others they are in parables.... (Luke 8:9-10a)

*And they were afraid, and they marveled,
saying to one another, "Who then is this, that
he commands even winds and water, and they
obey him?"* (Luke 8:25)

*But they did not understand this saying, and
it was concealed from them, so that they
might not perceive it. And they were afraid to
ask him about this saying.* (Luke 9:45)

*John answered, "Master, we saw someone
casting out demons in your name, and we
tried to stop him, because he does not follow
with us." But Jesus said to him, "Do not stop
him, for the one who is not against you is for
you."* (Luke 9:49-50)

From these few passages we can see Luke identify
when the disciples were mistaken or misunderstood about
what Jesus said. Hence, arguing that Jesus meant something
other than buying a real sword is an argument with no support—even indirect support. The clearer and more direct in-
terpretation of Luke 22 is that Jesus was preparing them for
travel without his presence and protection. A normal and
necessary part of travel was providing a safeguard against
attack along the roadway.

10. Question or Objection: Can a Christian husband defend his wife from a deadly assault by using lethal
force?

*Husbands, love your wives, as Christ loved
the church and gave himself up for her.... In
the same way husbands should love their
wives as their own bodies. He who loves his
wife loves himself. For no one ever hated his*

174

own flesh, but nourishes and cherishes it, just as Christ does the church, because we are members of his body. (Eph. 5:25; 28-30)

But if anyone does not provide for his relatives, and especially for members of his household, he has denied the faith and is worse than an unbeliever. (1 Tim. 5:8)

Response: Yes. Scripture clearly teaches that husbands are absolutely called to willingly lay down their own lives for their wives and children. Ephesians 5:25 commands husbands to love their wives "as Christ loved the church and gave himself up for her." Being willing to die for our families is a Christ-like attribute we hold dearly. However, allowing an assailant to kill us without stopping them does nothing to ultimately protect our loved ones. Paul continues in Ephesians to exhort husbands to care for their wives as they do their own bodies. Using physical and lethal force when reasonable and necessary is going to protect your family far more than throwing yourself in the line of fire only to leave your widow defenseless and without your love and caring.

God instituted human government to rule and protect human life. Police and military are duly commissioned to carry out that charge. God commissioned husbands to protect their wives and parents to protect their children. Thankfully in America, the government understands the necessity to allow its citizens the right to act upon those commissions. God likewise urged all believers to stand up for the rights of the innocent. Again, our government has provided us with legal means to protect and safeguard innocent others from physical harm, and if necessary by the use of lethal force.

11. Question or Objection: Isn't the unique calling of the Church to live in reliance upon heavenly protection and not on armed defense?

God is our refuge and strength, a very present help in trouble. (Ps. 46:1)

And my God will supply every need of yours according to his riches in glory in Christ Jesus. (Phil. 4:19)

You will be hated by all for my name's sake. But not a hair of your head will perish. (Luke 21:17-18)

Response: No, the unique calling of the Church is not to live in reliance upon heavenly protection. The unique calling of the Church is to take the gospel to the world (see the Great Commandment, Matt. 28:18-20). That being said, nowhere are we ordained to do so by the use of lethal force. However, the discussion about the use of lethal force for self-defense must not be conflated with government oppression to stop the gospel message. Neither should it be confused with revenge or retaliation. Throughout human history God's people used a balanced approach to self-defense.

Christians live in a world where we are expected to provide for our own physical wellbeing. We pray to the Lord that he will provide our daily bread, and then we go to work to earn money to buy food. When health issues plague us, we pray for healing and seek medical help. We invest, save, and plan financially for the future and ask God to protect our money. This is a balanced approach. It's trusting God and taking responsible action. Why would we approach our physical safety and the physical safety of our families any differently?

Appendix A
The New FBI Qualification Course

- Target used is the QIT-99
- Course consists of a total of 60 rounds
- Each round counts as one point
- Any hits inside the target area count
- You must draw from concealment for every string of shots
- Passing score for Agents is 48 out of 60

Stage 1: 3 yard line

- 3 rounds in 3 seconds using your strong hand only
- 3 rounds in 3 seconds using your strong hand only
- 3 rounds using strong hand only, switch hands, 3 rounds using support hand only all in 8 seconds

Total of 12 rounds for Stage 1

Stage 2: 5 yard line

From here on out, all shooting is done with two hands

- 3 rounds in 3 seconds
- 3 rounds in 3 seconds
- 3 rounds in 3 seconds
- 3 rounds in 3 seconds

Total of 12 rounds for Stage 2

Stage 3: 7 yard line

- 4 rounds in 4 seconds
- 4 rounds in 4 seconds

- Have two magazines loaded with four rounds each. Fire four rounds, reload, fire another four rounds in 8 seconds.

Total of 16 rounds for Stage 3

Stage 4: 15 yard line

- 3 rounds in 6 seconds
- 3 rounds in 6 seconds
- 4 rounds in 8 seconds

Total of 10 rounds for Stage 4

Stage 5: 25 yard line

This stage involves the use of a barricade/cover)

- Move to cover and fire 2 rounds standing, then 3 rounds kneeling all in 15 seconds
- Move to cover and fire 2 rounds standing, then 3 rounds kneeling all in 15 seconds

Total of 10 rounds for Stage 5

Source: USA Carry, http://www.usacarry.com/new-fbi-qualification-course/, accessed December 12, 2015.

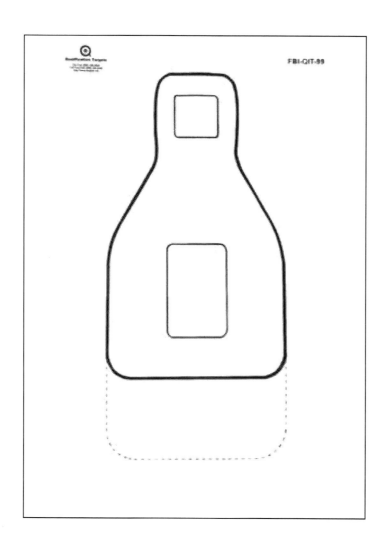

Works Cited

Anderson, W. F. (2006). *Forensic Analysis.* Boulder: Paladin Press.

Artwohl, A. (2002, October). Perceptual and Memory Distortion During Officer-Involved Shootings. *FBI Law Enforcement Bulletin*, 18-24.

Basic Pistol Course, National Rifle Association. (2009). *NRA Basic Pistol Shooting Course.* Fairfax, VA: NRA Training Department.

Biblical Studies Press, L.L.C. (1996-2006). *Holy Bible, New English Translation.* Richardson: Biblical Studies Press, L.L.C.

Blue Letter Bible. (n.d.). Retrieved from http://www.blueletterbible.org/index.cfm

Bonneville County Sheriff's Office. (2013). Active Shooter Training. Idaho Falls, ID, USA.

Brotherhood Mutual. (2015). *Brotherhood Mutual Insurance Company.* Retrieved December 28, 2015, from Safety Library, Church and Armed Security Guards: http://www.brotherhoodmutual.com/index.cfm/resources/ministry-safety/article/should-churches-have-armed-security-guards/

Cable News Network. (2015, October 2). *CNN News.* Retrieved December 5, 2015, from Oregon shooting: Gunman dead after college rampage: http://www.cnn.com/2015/10/01/us/oregon-college-shooting/index.html

Carson, D. (1991). *Pillar New Testament Commentary, John.* Grand Rapids: Wm. B. Eerdmans Publishing Company.

Carter, J. A., Maher, S., & and Neumann, P. R. (2014). *#Greenbirds: Measuring Importance and Influence in Syrian Foreign Fighter Networks.* London: The International Centre for the Study of Radicalisation and Political Violence.

Chinn, C. (2012). *Evil Invades Sancuary.* Carl Chinn.

Chinn, C. (2016). *Ministry Violence Statistics.* Retrieved from Security? In Church?: http://www.carlchinn.com/Church_Security_Concepts.html

Cooper, J. (1972). *Principles of Personal Defense.* Boulder: Paladin Press.

Ellis, R., Payne, E., Perez, E., & Ford, D. (2015, June 18). *Shooting suspect in custody after Charleston church massacre.* Retrieved January 30, 2016, from Cable News Network: http://www.cnn.com/2015/06/18/us/charleston-south-carolina-shooting/index.html

ESPN Sports. (2012, 12 12). A Football Life. *Marcus Allen.* USA: ESPN.

Farlex Partner Medical Dictionary. (2012). *The Free Dictionary*. Retrieved December 23, 2015, from Medical Dictionary: http://medical-dictionary.thefreedictionary.com/phobia

Federal Bureau of Investigation, Critical Incident Response Group. (n.d.). *Active Shooter Incidents*. Retrieved from Federal Bureau of Investigation: https://www.fbi.gov/about-us/office-of-partner-engagement/active-shooter-incidents

Federal Emergency Management Agency. (2013). *Guide for Developing High-Quality Emergency Operations Plans for Houses of Worship.* US Department of Homeland Security. Washington: US Department of Homeland Security.

Fox News. (2016, March Monday). *U.S. Home*. Retrieved 2016, from Foxnews.com: http://www.foxnews.com/us/2016/03/07/idaho-pastor-shot-day-after-praying-at-ted-cruz-rally.html

Furguson, S. B. (1988). *The Sermon on the Mount.* Edinburgh: Banner of Truth.

Gorka, S. L., & Gorka, K. C. (2015). *ISIS: The Threat to the United States.* McLean: Threat Knowledge Group.

Grossman, D. (1995). The Bullet Proof Mind audio seminar.

Grossman, D. (1996). *On Killing.* US: Back Bay Books.

Grossman, D. (2008). *On Combat.* US: Warrior Science Publications.

Hanson, J. (2013, May 31). *USA Carry.* Retrieved December 12, 2015, from The New FBI Qualification Course: http://www.usacarry.com/new-fbi-qualification-course/

Hicks, M. (2016, February 6). *Feds: Dearborn Hts. man supports ISIS, planned attack.* Retrieved February 20, 2016, from The Detriot News: http://www.detroitnews.com/story/news/local/wayne-county/2016/02/05/feds-dearborn-hts-man-supports-isis-planned-attack/79906302/

Jordan, B. (1965). *No Second Place Winner.* Concord, NH, USA: Police Bookshelf.

Kernan, K. (2015, December 7). *New York Post.* Retrieved December 11, 2015, from nypost.com: http://nypost.com/2015/12/07/stephen-currys-brilliance-all-starts-with-some-imagination/

Lewinski, B. (2002, November/December). Biomechanics of Lethal Force Encounters-- Officer Movements. *The Police Marksman*, pp. 19-23.

Lewinski, B. (2005, August 10). *PoliceOne.com.* Retrieved December 11, 2015, from PoliceOne.com: http://www.policeone.com/officer-shootings/articles/117909-Study-reveals-important-truths-hidden-in-the-details-of-officer-involved-shootings/

Merriam-Webster. (2011). *Merriam-Webster.com.* Retrieved April 1, 2011, from Merriam-Webster: www.merriam-webster.com/dictionary/justified

Merriam-Webster. (2015). *Merriam-Webster Online Dictionary.* Retrieved October 23, 2015, from Dictionary: http://www.merriam-webster.com/dictionary/sanctuary

Murray, K. (2016, March 9). Personal Correspondance by email.

Murray, K. R. (2004). *Training at the Speed of Life, Vol. 1.* Gotha: Armiger Publications, Inc.

National Fire Protection Association. (2015, December 4). *Religious and funeral properties.* Retrieved from The National Fire Protection Association: http://www.nfpa.org/research/reports-and-statistics/fires-by-property-type/assemblies/religious-and-funeral-properties

National Fire Protection Association. (2015, December 4). *School fires with 10 or more deaths*. Retrieved from The National Fire Protection Association: http://www.nfpa.org/research/reports-and-statistics/fires-by-property-type/educational/school-fires-with-10-or-more-deaths

News 12 KXII staff reporters. (2005, August 31). *Church Shootings - 911 Call For Help*. Retrieved December 5, 2015, from KXII.com: http://www.kxii.com/home/headlines/1709036.html

Police Executive Research Forum. (2014). *The Police Response to Active Shooter Incidents*. Washington: Police Executive Research Forum.

Rainer, T. (2015, December 16). *16 Trends in American Churches in 2016 (Part 1)*. Retrieved January 29, 2016, from CP Opinion: http://www.christianpost.com/news/16-trends-american-churches-2016-part-1-152468/#JMDQgpJ0dbaHgK82.99

Steffan, M. (2013, January 30). *Christianity Today*. Retrieved January 28, 2015, from Christianity Today.com: http://www.christianitytoday.com/gleanings/2013/january/deaths-from-church-attacks-rise-36-in-2012.html

Stuart, D. K. (2006). *The New American Commentary, Exodus, Vol. 2.* B&H Publishing Group: Nashville.

Texas State University and Federal Bureau of Investigation. (2014). *A Study of Active Shooter Incidents in the United States Between 2000 and 2013.* Washington: U.S. Department of Justice.

The Editors of Encyclopædia Britannica. (2015). *Hazael, King of Damascus.* Retrieved from Encyclopedia Britannnica: http://www.britannica.com/biography/Hazael

The Federal Bureau of Investigation. (2015). *Frequently Asked Questions.* Retrieved from FBI.gov: https://www.fbi.gov/about-us/faqs

The National Rifle Association. (2012). *Basic Personal Protection in the Home Course.* Fairfax: The National Rifle Association of America.

The Physics Classroom. (1996-2015). *Kinetic Energy.* Retrieved January 15, 2016, from The Physics Classroom: http://www.physicsclassroom.com/Class/energy/u5l1c.cfm

USA Today Network and KGW Staff. (2015, October 14). *http://www.cnn.com/2015/10/01/us/oregon-college-shooting/index.html.* Retrieved

December 5, 2015, from KGW.com:
http://www.kgw.com/story/news/local/roseburg-college-shooting/2015/10/02/hero-shot-7-times-standing-up-roseburg-shooter/73205662/

Wood, M. (2013). *Newhall Shooting: A tactical analysis.* Iola, WI, USA: Gun Digest Books.

About the Author

 Tim Rupp's law enforcement career spans four decades. His father was both a career military man and pastor, so it was natural for Tim to enlist in the Air Force after graduating high school in 1979. Tim served four years active duty as an Air Force law enforcement specialist. After his enlistment, Tim joined the San Antonio Police Department (SAPD) and gave 24 years of dedicated service before retiring in 2007. During his SAPD career he worked as a patrol officer, homicide detective, patrol sergeant, sex crimes sergeant, police academy supervisor, and internal affairs sergeant-investigator. Tim certified as a police firearms instructor and supervised police firearms and tactics for several years. He continues to serve with the Bonneville County Sheriff's Office as a reserve deputy.

Before retiring from the police department, Tim was called to pastor Elm Creek Baptist Church in La Vernia, TX, just outside of San Antonio. After retiring from the police department he was called to pastor fulltime in Idaho. Tim currently serves as senior pastor at River of Life Church in Idaho Falls, teaches firearms with his son, and instructs online for Crown College. He graduated from Texas State University (Master of Science in Criminal Justice), Southwestern Baptist Theological Seminary (Master of Divinity and MACE), and Western Seminary (Doctor of Ministry). Tim is married to Sherry and they have three children, Christina, Aaron, and Emily and four grandchildren (with more on the way!).

Made in the USA
Lexington, KY
25 March 2017